THE INSIDE STORY OF

THE AMERICAN HOME

MYRNA KAYE

A Bulfinch Press Book • Little, Brown and Company • Boston • New York • Toronto • London

Research Assistant and Illustrations Editor: Karen D. Fischer

First edition

Library of Congress Cataloging-in-Publication Data

Kaye, Myrna.

    There's a bed in the piano : the inside story of the American home

/ Myrna Kaye.—1st ed.

      p.   cm.

    "A Bulfinch Press book."

    Includes bibliographical references and index.

    ISBN 0-8212-2374-7

    1. Furniture—United States.   2. Architecture, Domestic—United States.   3. Interior decoration—United States.   I. Title.

NK2405.K39   1998

749.213—dc21   97-51321

Bulfinch Press is an imprint and trademark of Little, Brown and Company (Inc.)

Published simultaneously in Canada by Little, Brown & Company (Canada) Limited

Designed by Caroline Rowntree

PRINTED IN SPAIN

D.L.TO:1044-1998

CONTENTS

ACKNOWLEDGMENTS

Among the experts whose knowledge made this book possible, none has been as important as Robert F. Trent, a scholar and sharer without peer who read the entire manuscript. (I made changes afterward, so he is blameless.) Experts who read chapters were Sara Chase, Preservation Consultant; Anne A. Grady; Dean Lahikainen, Peabody Essex Museum; Gerald W. R. Ward, Museum of Fine Arts, Boston; and Philip Zea, Historic Deerfield. Were it not for their comments, accuracy would have suffered. Joan Lautman, Roberta Leviton, Sabra Morton, Patricia Warner, and Richmond Warner read chapters as "typical readers." Each is so astute that there is nothing typical about any of them.

Tom Savage, Historic Charleston Foundation; Stephen Patrick, Hammond-Harwood House, Annapolis; and Richard Nylander, Society for the Preservation of New England Antiquities (SPNEA), shared fawbits they had collected.

Many others helped this book to be, including Rodris Roth, Domestic Life Collection, Smithsonian Institution; Lorna Condon, Library and Archives, SPNEA; Jonathan Fairbanks, Museum of Fine Arts, Boston; Alan Miller; Jane Hageman, Elisabeth D. Garrett, Peter Gittleman, Royall House; William Hosley, Wadsworth Atheneum, and Richard Dabrowski, Shaker Workshops, helped us gather images. Barbara Williams performed a thousand chores; Suzanne Hurst and Kiki Sansalone translated other languages, as did Arisa Tsutsui, of Tokushima, Japan.

Janet Bush, my editor, Ann Eiselein, her assistant, and Luise Erdmann, my copy editor, had faith and patience and diligence. Caroline Rowntree, the book's designer, deserves much of the credit for what you see here. Jonathan Nerenberg performed the wonder of drawing what I saw in my mind's eye. The text is more readable because of the editing comments of friends and fellow writers who read the manuscript: Barbara Mende, Shirley Moskow, Jeri Quinzio, and Rose Yesu.

My patient husband and aide extraordinaire, Murray Kaye, is the person without whom this book would not be.

My greatest appreciation goes to Karen Fischer—and her tolerant husband, Joe. As illustrations editor, Karen traveled, studied, looked, wrote, telephoned, and tracked. Dauntless in the pursuit of the best and most appropriate, she discovered wonderful objects, pictures, and photographs that not only perfectly suited my ideas and text but also kept the book to a size that you can read in bed. In any bed.

INTRODUCTION

This book invites the reader to cross American thresholds, survey the rooms, and look at the furniture. Much of our country's story is found there. Homes are such exciting social documents that most of us, without study or expertise, routinely pick up some of their messages. As an archaeologist reads pot shards, we read objects.

The furniture and rooms in American homes—readable bits of our history—tell us about individuals, whence they came and where and how they lived. We can read chairs and see a history of changing lifestyles. We can see two chairs attesting to two different eras, or to the same era in different places, or to the same place and time but different economic levels, or to the different personal tastes of neighbors, or to different ideas of beauty, even to different modes of sitting and different concepts of comfort. We can read tables to see how high people sat, what they drank, with whom they traded, and what they admired.

Historians commonly study historic ob-jects. Some of us discern history more easily in cocktail tables and rocking chairs than in cannons and battleships. While ordinary objects speak of people and their attitudes and circumstances, American households as a whole speak of our national character. The academic discipline is called "material culture." People imbue their objects with their most fundamental beliefs, so American objects are American ideas in tangible form.

We, however, have to know what we are looking at and in what context to place it, so this book is a practical how-to: how to read rooms and furniture, how to put American objects in perspective, how to see the home as a historic cultural document. This how-to is for anyone curious about American life. Our homes are American not only because of where they are but also because we are a distinctive people. We live in diverse regions but have forged a national identity that reflects our diversity. In the course of our history, this cross-cultural society developed a peculiarly

American culture that can be read in mansions and hovels, apartments and houses, past and present, in every part of the nation.

However, readers of homes need caveats when they interpret the familiar, so this book serves as a road map with danger signs posted along the way. To warn the reader of misinterpretations, misnomers, and myths, I include them but flag them for what they are. For years I kept a file on the myths I heard from antiques dealers, writers, house guides, and historians. To label the file, I coined the term "fawbit": **f**ictional **a**ccount **w**ithout **b**asis **i**n **t**ruth. Whenever I recount one of these flights of fancy in this book, I brand it in bold type: **fawbit.**

Some stories are not actually fawbits but can be misleading if not placed in context. For example, one story tells of the tall legs of a high chest being "ruthlessly amputated" just to fit the chest into a low-ceilinged room. The account can mislead a reader who does not know just how common the story was and how common leg problems were. The storytellers have not said that such legs were prone to damage, that they split with age, and that many succumbed to woodworm and therefore were cut.

The tale of the capricious owner with low ceilings is informative, however. It was current during the Colonial Revival, usually well after the supposed "surgery," and was told by enthusiasts of colonial designs who were ridiculing the preceding generation for undervaluing their old things. Phrases like "ruthlessly amputated" are warning signs. In watching out for them and listening to stories skeptically, we can

get the right messages. We can distinguish fact from fawbit. A bonus from misinformation is that we gain an understanding of a later era, such as a view of the late-nineteenth-century Colonial Revival in the tale of an eighteenth-century colonial high chest.

Objects tell honest stories of their time: antiques, if authentic, speak of periods past. Reproductions and fraudulent objects, like fawbits, tell of the time they were made. In writing about antique American furniture in *Fake, Fraud, or Genuine?*, I gave hints and clues that helped separate the spurious from the authentic. Authenticity is important because the cultural information we want is in each object itself. We glean it by looking. We can see construction and understand the maker. We can see elegance or simplicity and learn something of the consumer.

The chapters in this history are, therefore, not chronological but thematic. Each follows a theme or a type of object rather than the calendar. Yet there are elements of the usual sort of history. The reading of objects is enhanced when it is augmented or clarified by additional history: social, craft, economic, personal, and cultural. I quote diaries, letters, and inventories of household goods prepared for probate courts, written documents that help to put the objects in historical perspective. A line in a 1733 inventory of the objects in a bedchamber—"144 p⁵ˢ [pieces] of Glass Ware on the Chest of Draws"—helps us envision the flat-top high chest playing its role of display shelf.

I tell about makers and owners. Craftsmen, through their crafts, their materials, and their design vocabularies, gave the objects their form. The owners and users gave them additional meaning, even cultural significance. When Thor and Margit Dahl brought a lavishly painted trunk with them from Norway in 1880 to beautify their new home, they also helped to transplant a Scandinavian painted tradition in America. We look at individuals and groups and see how their ideas of home were carried to America and across the land. Because Americans came from all over, so did American ideas.

Here we became a distinct people. We speak English but are not English. When we borrowed the English Windsor chair, we changed it. We are a nation of nomads who are still carriers of designs and objects. This book highlights things we adopted or rejected, or accepted only after adapting it for ourselves. It also includes some American ideas we have exported.

Our style of domestic life came from indigenous peoples, early settlers, slaves, and later immigrants. Each had a rich heritage, and Americans exchanged traditions among themselves. Modifications began upon arrival, even though change is difficult and people change things only for compelling reasons. By keeping our eye on changes, we see what is essentially American. Soon after landing in this richly timbered land, we reworked designs and techniques developed in wood-poor lands. For example, American pine is what changed the Windsor chair. An abundance of furniture woods led Americans to create shapes that proclaimed what then seemed true: "We have wood to waste."

Although the chapters are not chronological, time is a big factor in this story. We see America change with time. The six drawers of my grandmother's bureau, once ideal for five, came to be ideal for one. My grandmother ascribed that to America. The same credit could be given to much else in this book, including the bed in the piano.

That object in the title, the subject at the core of the first chapter, may tickle our sensibilities today because the purposes of the one piece of furniture seem incongruous. The goal of putting a bed in a piano seems too ambitious. Current perceptions are part of what this book is about. Another part is the way an object or room affected people when it was new. Comparing the two is seeing history at work.

Sometimes people change the shape of things; sometimes they don't. Why American furniture and rooms had the forms they did is part of this story. The famous FFF rule of design—"form follows function"—is alliterative and memorable but falls short. To say simply that an object assumed a form to fill its functions does not explain why a bed was hidden away in a piano. Form follows several factors, each a part of a culture's story. Factors that augment the FFF rule are the maker's skill, the properties of the construction material, and the history of the form itself.

The first three chapters focus on crafts, craftsmen, and their materials. They also take the crafts as points of departure. We look at how objects went from the simple to the complex by looking at cases (Chapter 1), from the regal to the relaxed, commonplace, and democratic while looking at chairs (Chapter 2), and from the stiff to the comfortable, looking at more seating (Chapter 3).

Distinctively American traditions are visible in our homes. We trace our unique experiences with security, openness, and privacy as we examine our public faces and visit our private nooks. We search for the origins of our open spaces (Chapter 4), look at the causes and consequences of opening walls (Chapter 5), and watch as, with walls, we create diverse and special spaces (Chapter 6).

In population, we are a nation of many nations; in design, a place of many places (Chapter 7). Reading our stylistic choices reveals much about this country.

Sometimes it seems that mysterious influences are at work in determining the designs that appeal to us, the furniture we choose, the rooms we want to live in. In this book we focus on an international exchange of that very sort, a Chinese aesthetic that seemed to waft in with the aroma of tea (Chapter 8).

The book concludes with messages from our homes (Chapter 9)—some that I have read in objects, some that other people have read. More of the story may be written by the reader who puts this book to use and reads additional objects and other rooms or reads them in new ways.

Source notes appear near the end of the book. They and the index may prove especially helpful when we return to eyewitness accounts from Jasper Danckaerts, a Dutchman visiting in 1680; Harriet Manigault, a young woman writing in Pennsylvania in the early 1800s;

Harriet Martineau, a visitor from England between 1834 and 1836; and Frederick Law Olmsted, a traveler in the South in the 1850s. We revisit Daniel Howard, a seventeenth-century blacksmith, and Jonathan Sayward, an eighteenth-century judge. Full citations for the illustrations, including the museum accession number where relevant, are in the illustration credits at the back of the book. Abbreviated credits appear in the captions.

Americans have been looking at antique objects for a long time. Antiquarians may have lovingly collected relics as homage to the famous or to ancestors, but we are indebted because they preserved the things we enjoy and read. So did collectors, for whom anything redolent of the past was worthy. We are their beneficiaries even if some of them, as during the Colonial Revival, clouded the picture with fawbits, fakes, and misleading histories. If art historians, researchers, and scholars seem to dwell on nuances in cabrioles and construction details in cornices, they also authenticate the objects we read, place them in context, and verify their stories.

Americans, curious about the rich and famous, also have an unusual interest in ordinary folk. British scholars began to study their vernacular furniture only after American furniture researchers, studying our vernacular design, asked about related English examples. Until then, objects just beneath the noses of astute design historians remained below their line of sight as they concentrated on the elegant fashions of the social elite. Our focus on the ordinary American changed that. Having learned so much from British scholars over the years, American scholars repaid the debt by pointing them in a new direction.

Here and there I cite relevant readings in the text, but I include no bibliography. I recommend *Decorative Arts and Household Furnishings in America 1620–1920, An Annotated Bibliography*, edited by Kenneth L. Ames and Gerald W. R. Ward (Winterthur, Del.: Winterthur Museum, 1989). It is excellent and inclusive. I also recommend the bibliographies in the following books, all excellent sources: Oscar P. Fitzgerald, *Four Centuries of American Furniture*; Jonathan L. Fairbanks and Elizabeth B. Bates, *American Furniture: 1620 to the Present*, which has a bibliography by Wendell Garrett and Allison Eckardt; and Edgar de N. Mayhew and Minor Myers, Jr., *A Documentary History of American Interiors from the Colonial Era to 1915*. The texts and illustrations in these books also merit reading. Mayhew and Myers has a list of museums with major furniture collections as well. Elisabeth Donaghy Garrett, *At Home: The American Family 1750–1870*, has a fine selective bibliography; the book is fascinating and comprehensive. And read anything by the English furniture historian John Gloag.

Harold L. Peterson, *Americans at Home*, and William Seale, *The Tasteful Interlude: American Interiors Through the Camera's Eye, 1860–1917*, have no bibliographies but are excellent resources. Although limited to New England from 1760 to 1860, Jane C. Nylander, *Our Own Snug Fireside*, is a fine resource with a worthwhile bibliography. *American Furniture*, edited by Luke Beckerdite, an annual journal first published in 1993, includes complete bibliographies of new publications. Its carefully focused articles, often argumentative but usually illuminating, are aimed at what Beckerdite aptly calls "object literacy." This journal is a great addition to a rather new discipline. Its fine illustrations are sometimes more easily read than some texts—but "object literacy" is its goal.

In recent years, we have benefited from much new scholarship and numerous books based on detailed studies of American furniture and interiors. Some specialize in regional styles, others in particular eras, particular forms, or specific collections; most are superbly illustrated. This book strives to build on them and widen the scene to look at America from coast to coast, to incorporate influences worldwide, to look at Americans over the centuries, and to include us all. Economic diversity and ethnic inclusiveness may be the politically correct fashion, but it is also faithful to American society.

The reader who crosses thresholds to look at rooms and read the furniture finds surprising expressions of American culture. A bed in a piano is just the beginning.

Olav Luraas, its splendid rosemaling (colorful painting of usually floral, sometimes floridly baroque, designs) makes it clear that this trunk was to do more than carry the Dahls' possessions; it was to beautify their new home.

The Dahls' 1868 trunk, as was typical of trunks of its era, had a rounded top. Only four changes have been made in the basic shape of trunks, the last two since the mid-nineteenth century. For craftsmen, change decreases efficiency; for their customers, change decreases familiarity. People usually want things to look "the way they always did." The past is such a power in the form of things that people change furniture shapes no more than they must.

By clinging to its ancient shape, people inadvertently preserved the forgotten history of the trunk. The form of the first trunk was dictated by the log from which it was made. The easiest way for someone to conceptualize making furniture was probably to create it by subtraction, taking away material, rather than by adding or constructing from parts. Therefore the log. Wood could be readily chipped or burned away, and a tree trunk was large enough for the subtraction method. The first furniture maker needed to find a suitable length of log, split it open, and hollow it out. The tools for such woodworking may well have been among the objects later carried and stored in it.

The split-off portion could be bound on as the top of the trunk, yielding a covered container that looked like a tree trunk—round all around, except at each end. Placed on the ground, the trunk would have rolled, so the first change to its appearance must have come

proceeded on foot while hired teams and teamsters hauled their large trunks. Failing to find the Skunk River, the route to the settlement of New Sweden at Brush Creek, Iowa, they followed the Des Moines River to Des Moines, then a fort and a few cabins. From there they moved past settled Indians and traveling Indians to a place where one lone white man, a hunter, lived. It was late September. Four families stayed there and founded Swede Point, Iowa, since renamed Madrid. The rest went on to the older settlement. No wonder that in 1869 Oliver Stephenson, writing from yet another settlement in Iowa, advised his parents in Sweden to emigrate in the spring and cautioned: "Don't bring heavy trunks, but have them as light as possible, well roped, and double locked."[4]

Thor and Margit Dahl brought a trunk (fig. 1.7) with them from Norway to Minneapolis in 1880. Decorated, signed, and dated twelve years earlier in Telemark by its painter, early in its history when the bottom was worked flat to make the trunk stand firm. When the flat-bottomed trunk was placed in a cave or other dwelling, it created a space within a space, a distinct place for storage.

The second change in the shape of trunks came much later. The backs of trunks were flattened so they would fit flush to the wall after they moved into dwellings with flat walls—stone castles, wooden houses. In the Middle Ages, trunks stood firm on the floor and flat against the wall, but many remained rounded in front and on top. That was true even of trunks no longer made of hollowed logs. Because familiar furniture shapes simply endure, the nineteenth-century trunk on the back of a Conestoga wagon heading west was rounded both on top and on the façade, vestiges of its prehistoric origin.

Not until the mid-nineteenth century was the trunk façade routinely made flat. This third change enabled more trunks to fit into the holds of steamships, hence the term "steamer trunk." Shortly thereafter, to allow trunks to be piled one upon another in railroad baggage cars, the tops were made flat—the fourth change.

So the trunks that furnished the dwellings at Swede Point in 1846 and the 1868 rose-maled trunk that enlivened the Dahls' home in Minneapolis were rounded on top. Even at the end of the nineteenth century, curved trunk lids persisted. In 1897, Sears, Roebuck offered nineteen trunks for sale. Twelve had flat tops, but five of them hinted at the ancient curve in gently rounded edges at the front and back of the lid. Four trunks had "barrel stave" tops (called "turtle backs" by antiques dealers)—lids rounded fore and aft and sloping at the sides. Two, including Sears's least expensive model, had rounded tops.

Flat tops gave trunks a new function. Collegians and campers used them as tables as well as storage cases. At home, trunks found prominent locations at the foot of the bed and in front of the sofa. In the 1980s, brass-covered trunks served as tables for the living room. Girding in brass was not new: trunks had metal coverings, bindings, and ornamentation from their beginning. Metal bindings made it possible to lock the trunk and helped keep the hollowed log intact as the wood shrank and cracked.

People wanted all, even common, rudimentary furniture to enhance their surroundings. On trunks, the metal bindings were decoratively worked; locks provided ornament as well as security. The art of decorative metalwork thrived over millennia in the binding of

Figure 1.8. Cradle, leather-covered wood, brass nails, New York, 1762. Made for the Brinckerhoff family. (Metropolitan Museum of Art.) Eighteenth-century leather-covered cradles were made in Boston and New York. Their shape and decoration were basically that of a trunk, nailing and all.

American board chests are closer to medieval European plank chests. Europeans, however, used thick planks, giving their carvers greater depth of material. American sawmills—some fifty were working in New England by 1675, cutting the broad timbers of the virgin forests—produced relatively thin sawn boards.[9] Wood and technology thus gave seventeenth-century American craftsmen a thinner material that lent itself to flatter surfaces. Ever since, heavily carved furniture has been the exception in America, often seeming redolent of other traditions.

In seventeenth-century American houses, small six-board boxes provided safe storage for documents and books. Some Puritan households contained only one book, the Bible, which proved excuse enough for nineteenth-century antiquarians to dub them "Bible boxes." Board boxes and board chests were often described by their wood, such as Howard's "deale Board Chest." "Deal" denoted a soft wood, probably white pine if the chest was made in America or, if Howard brought the chest from England, a European pine or fir. Our first **fawbit,** or fictional **a**ccount **w**ithout **b**asis **i**n **t**ruth, was told to me by a tour guide in Savannah: "Deal desks are so called because merchants signed deals on them." Like all fawbits, this one deals in misinformation.

Small board boxes usually sat on larger boxes and therefore could be made without feet. Large boxes and chests, however, required feet to lift the bottom off the damp floor, thereby discouraging vermin and inhibiting decay to the chest bottom and to the contents. Nevertheless, so many seventeenth-century board chests succumbed to the damp that one cannot judge their popularity by the number of surviving examples. A carpenter making a six-board chest furnished it with feet easily. He cut the sides of the chest long and notched them at the base (see fig. 1.4a). Howard's board chest may have stood on feet created by a simple chevron notch.

A desk was a board box whose lid was on a slant. Slanted boards had been writing desks in the Middle Ages, the slope providing a scribe with an inclined writing surface. The desks of seventeenth-century Americans were small, nailed, slant-lid boxes. When large desks became popular in the eighteenth century, the slanted lid remained, even though it was above a stack of wide bureau drawers and was no longer the writing surface (fig. 1.10). The

Figure 1.10. Desk, mahogany and white pine, H: 44″; W: 41½″; D: 22″. Henry Rust, Salem, Massachusetts, 1760–1800. (Bernard & S. Dean Levy.) We no longer wrote on its slanted surface, yet we expected a desk to have a canted lid.

canted lid on such so-called fall-front or slant-lid desks opened to reveal small drawers and pigeonholes hidden within; when folded out, its inner surface formed a horizontal writing shelf. One might wonder why, if colonial merchants were going to write on the horizontal, cabinetmakers kept setting the lid on a slant. They retained it for a century because a sloped lid said "desk" to all who saw it.

Wealthy colonials enjoyed an elaborate form of desk, a statuesque case that combined a bookcase with doors above a fall-front desk, a form that remained in fashion into the nineteenth century (see the case at the left, fig. 8.8). Many a prosperous business was run at home from a tall black walnut or mahogany secretary, often called a "scrutoire." The two-part secretary—cubby-holed desk and ledger-filled bookcase—was a big step toward the Wooton desk and corporate headquarters.

PUTTING IT TOGETHER

Small seventeenth-century desk boxes and large eighteenth-century scrutoires were both of board construction. The fastening, however, changed. In the seventeenth century, Americans usually nailed boards together (often with wooden nails). In the eighteenth and thereafter, they cut rows of the tail-shaped notches along the edges of the boards and meshed the dovetailed ends together, locking the edges of boards together without nails (fig. 1.11). They adopted this technique as the seventeenth century waned, although Continental Europeans dovetailed boards together by 1510, when Marx Reichlich delineated a dovetailed edge on

Figure 1.11. Chest on frame with drawer, birch and yellow pine, H: 36³/₄"; W: 40³/₄"; D: 18". Probably by Micajah Buchanan (1804–1868), Sumter County, Georgia, 1845–1865.
(Atlanta History Center.)
The board construction of the upper case is evident in the row of twelve neat dovetails at each corner. The frame is joined.

a board-chest in his painting *The Birth of the Virgin.*[10]

Howard's "deale Board Chest," however, must have been nailed. When he died in 1675, the European craft had yet to thrive in England, let alone in America. Not until the end of the seventeenth century did English immigrant craftsmen bring their new technique to America. Soon cabinetmakers, as the practitioners of the craft of interlocking dovetails were known, wanted to hide the rows of dovetails that held their cases together. They covered the wood with veneers and inlays, giving the flat surfaces a dramatically new appearance. Using veneer, thin sheets of wood glued on the façades, cabinetmakers created patterns from the natural figure of the wood. With inlay, they formed geometric designs such as stars and shells by juxtaposing different woods. Cabinetmaking thrived as all sorts of board containers were dovetailed together and given dressy flat surfaces.

The look and craft of cabinetry, and the vogue for veneered decoration, came to Eng-

Figure 1.17. High chest, mahogany and white pine, H: 87¼"; W: 39"; D: 20⅜". John Townsend (paper label), Newport, Rhode Island, ca. 1760. (Museum of Fine Arts, Boston.) Placing two drawers on the top tier permitted an arrangement of the brasses that, along with the figure of the wood on the drawers, moves the viewer's eye up to the apex of the case. This great American high chest lost a finial in transit.

as icon. It was inspired by, and named for, a museum example (fig. 1.17) that was shipped from one museum to another for exhibition and lost a finial in transit.

Cederquist chose a form that in several ways epitomizes American conservatism in furniture design. High chests were the earliest cabinetry cases, the first chests of drawers. In America they remained stylish throughout the eighteenth century, long after they had become passé in England, whence they'd come.

In the early eighteenth century, high chests were favored by all who aspired to be gentle-

men. The earliest examples (see fig. 1.15) had flat tops and stood on table-like bases whose legs were so fragile that cabinetmakers' designs called for four legs across the front. The front of the base was designed as an arcade—four turned legs creating three arched spaces between. Above the three arches were three discrete areas, often drawers.

By the 1730s, turned legs were out: cabriole (S-curve) legs were in. The latter were integral to the base, making for a stronger structure, so two front legs sufficed. Yet rather than omit the two inner front legs, cabinetmakers at first merely replaced them with short turned pendants. Structurally useless, the remnants were for the observer's eyes, supplying turnings where they were expected.

Even after the pendants disappeared around midcentury, the lower tier of the façade retained its tripartite design. A central shell drawer flanked by boxy drawers was popular. The skirt between the two front legs kept the three arches that had been dictated by four front legs. The Newport high chest that was Cederquist's inspiration has a three-drawer lowest tier. Cederquist's high chest kept three arches there. A high chest made in America as the Revolution began had a three-part skirt only because four front legs had been necessary four generations before. That's being design-retentive.

Cederquist included glimpses of the Newport case that lost a part. He gleefully "deconstructed" the high chest into parts, as if each had been somehow separately crated. A Southern Californian who was born in 1946, he cre-

Figure 1.18. High chest
"Le Fleuron Manquant"
("The Missing Finial"),
birch plywood and other woods,
H: $78\frac{5}{8}$"; W: 35"; D: $12\frac{1}{2}$".
John Cederquist, Capistrano
Beach, California, 1989.
(Private collection / Museum of
Fine Arts, Boston.)

本物の暮らしやすさをあなたに。
国際水準の住まいを実現する東急ホーム〈ミルクリーク〉。

Cod. dormers and all (fig. 2.1). Beyond the threshold and the line of outdoor shoes, the seating, save that in perhaps one traditional room with tatami mats, was Western. With seats at chair height, the other furniture was also Western (specifically, American). The height of the accessories, artwork, and tables—all governed by the chair—were elevated. The entire kitchen, except for the inclusion of a deep fryer for tempura, could easily be taken for one in America. The counter heights and cooking equipment—the very ways the room functions—were based on the height of the seats and sitters. Seating furniture governs interiors.

READING CHAIRS

When curators and material culturists—people who read objects—read seating furniture, the stories are about the sitters. Cushions, rocking chairs, stools, and sofas all tell different stories. Even the arrangements of seating in a room are revealing. Changes in seating mark changes in posture, manners, and people's con-

cepts of themselves. Anyone who was surprised by the unisex appearance of clothing near the end of the twentieth century was not looking at chairs at midcentury, when the less imposing chairs known as "ladies' chairs" vanished from living room suites.

Readers of chairs need to know how a chair was read in its time. The chair that was America's greatest innovation in furniture—perhaps America's most potent impact on world culture until Levi's and jazz—was the rocking chair (fig. 2.2). Twentieth-century Americans read such chairs as "quaint and comfy," but at the beginning of the nineteenth century, having recently burst on the world scene, rocking chairs were "revolutionary and jarring." The very words "rocking chair" were an oxymoron to Europeans, to whom all chairs said "stability" and "rectitude." The chair, after all, descended from the throne, and colonial Americans lived under monarchs and understood the chair's royal connections. Many American chairs continued to resemble their regal ancestors, some more than others: armchairs more than side chairs, men's chairs more than women's chairs, rocking chairs least of all.

The ancient world had chair-sitters—the Egyptians, Assyrians, Greeks, and Romans (although Romans would lie on couches for dinner). Then, in the barbaric centuries, ages once called "Dark," chairs vanished along with all the other domestic furnishings save trunks and simple chests. Chair-sitting disappeared more quickly in the western reaches of the fallen Roman Empire than in Byzantium, which held on to amenities longer. One exceptional seat

Figure 2.2. Boston rocker, original paint, "H.K.K. and Co." inscribed in paint on seat bottom, New England, 1845–1875. (Society for the Preservation of New England Antiquities.)

Figure 2.3 *King David,* bas-relief, prayer room doorway, Sainte-Marie-de-la-Daurade, Toulouse, France, 1180–1196. (Musée des Augustins, Toulouse.) King David sits on an X-frame folding stool playing his harp. The crown and folding stool designated the figure a king; the harp designated him David.

survived—a portable throne. It was a mere stool, an X-frame with a leather slung seat, a sort of director's chair without back or arms. The medieval ruler might either sit like a director, his bottom cradled side to side, or with the seat slung fore and aft (fig. 2.3). Such was the throne of the Holy Roman Emperor. Later the X-frame gained a back and arms, and a king sat as directors do today.

Long before Charlemagne was crowned in A.D. 800, a simple, portable X-frame stool was recognized as a throne. Ancient Egyptians during the Middle Kingdom (2400–1580 B.C.) had the folding stool, each leg perhaps carved like a bird's long neck and head or to resemble an animal's leg and paw. Millennia later, the members of the X-frame, then called a "faldstool," were still being carved to look like birds' necks or animals' legs. Visiting English bishops used a faldstool as a throne away from home.

If that was a throne, what did other people sit on? In medieval castles, some sat on window seats built into the stone walls, cushions helping with the cold, hard seats. While an ornate bench with cushions before the fire suited a saint (see fig. 1.6: note also the low faldstool beneath her flowers), others sat on the simplest of backless plank benches or on the top of chests placed against the stone wall. To protect the sitter's back from the bitter cold of the stone, wooden wall paneling and textile wall coverings became fashionable, making stone interiors look more inviting. From the wooden wall paneling arose another type of throne.

In his own cathedral, the English bishop exchanged his portable X-frame throne for a more majestic one, one derived from the equation: chest + wall panel = seat. The lord of the castle or the manor had one too. This throne was a large joined box of a seat, with a high paneled back and lower paneled sides for armrests, very like the back and arms of fixed choir stalls. Thrones looked like interior woodwork because they began as interior woodwork. Their origin remained visible.

Throne furniture had to be able to move to approach the hearth, originally set in the middle of the floor, later moved against the wall. By attaching the paneling not to the wall but to the back of the box, joiners created a throne that could be liberated from the wall—furniture, not woodwork. The same evolution produced a settle, a backed bench that was often called a "settle bench." By the fourteenth century, a throne looked our image of a throne.

The joined chair in a seventeenth-century American home, often dubbed "Great," was somewhat smaller and less grandly carved but nevertheless a throne's look-alike (see fig. 1.4c). Its unyielding vertical back fostered—"forced," you might say after sitting in the chair—an erect posture that lent presence to the throne and sitter alike. A seventeenth-century joined chair was a dignified seat for a dignitary. By their lights, the heads of Puritan households merited thronelike seats, which says a lot about those sitters. And about the "Great" chair, even if it began as, and still resembled, a box shoved back against a paneled wall. Puritans sat proud and tall in great chairs.

A throne elevated the sitter above floor-sitters, and it often stood on a dais. Height equaled authority, so the king or lord sat above those aptly called the "lower" classes. Even the king's feet were elevated on a footstool. In 1650, Italian, French, and Spanish courtiers were walking around on high heels, inspired by privileged Venetian women whose elevated shoes placed them above their servants. Sitting tall was important in the seventeenth century.

Thrones and settles, although furniture, were barely movable. Two easily moved seats of the late medieval castle were in common use in seventeenth-century New England houses but do not survive: a plank bench and a stool on stick legs. These were ruder than the joiner's stool or bench (fig. 1.12). Joined seats were four-legged: their bases were like box frames. The plainer stool was a small, often round plank standing on stick legs, a utilitarian stool that was often three-legged.

Three-legged joined chairs were popular in Britain and permitted stability on uneven floors—especially important when the flooring was rare or poor. Who has not wobbled on a four-legged seat? The three-legged stool, the standard individual seat in the Middle Ages, took care of that.

Its seat was round probably because it descended from a tree trunk that was used as a stool. Swedish *kubbstols* and Norwegian *kubbestols*, versions of which Scandinavians continued to make after immigrating, were tree-trunk chairs.[3] *Kubb* meant "cob" or "lump"; a tree trunk was a lump for a seat. American *kubbestols* add an interesting note to

the saga of immigrants and furniture. Scandinavian-Americans enjoyed it all—the completely European: the Scandinavian trunks they brought with them (see fig. 1.7); the American: the beds they adopted on arrival; and the hybrid: chairs of a Scandinavian form made in America.

American seating has been surprisingly inclusive, and we have been more richly endowed by the long history of world furniture than our short span of years would suggest. The settlement in America came at a time that Europe was revolutionizing its seating, discarding the medieval and rediscovering furniture forms lost when the Roman Empire collapsed. England, our most direct source, lagged behind the Continent. The commonly held idea—that it took a long time for furniture designs to cross the Atlantic—is not true. Wealthy colonists quickly emulated the styles current among merchants in England; Europe's chair renaissance was slow to cross the Channel. After continuing quickly across the ocean, styles stopped for a long pause in America's coastal towns. Fashionable seating was slow to migrate inland.

TURNERS AND TURNING

The intricate embellishments that flourished on seventeenth-century colonial chairs came from yet another furniture craft, turning, or more accurately, perhaps, from yet another tool, the lathe.

The lathe merits our special attention, for this single tool was the basis of an entire craft (fig. 2.4). By dominating early colonial design, lathe work became emblematic of the era. Ul-

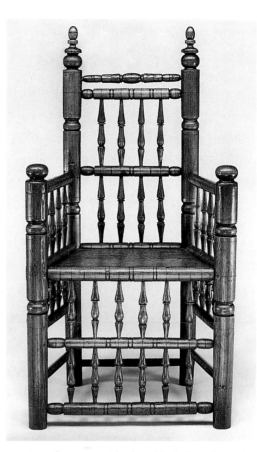

Figure 2.4 *The Turner,* engraving, Jan Joris van Vliet, Delft, Netherlands, ca. 1635. (Rijksmuseum.) Spinning wheel and slatback chair, two of the turner's products, stand in the shop as the lathe spins the wood by means of the overhead pole, foot treadle, and cord wrapped directly around the work.

Figure 2.5. Armchair, hickory and ash, H: 44¾"; W: 32½"; D: 15⅜". Coastal Massachusetts, ca. 1650. (Metropolitan Museum.) The turner's art at its best.

timately, the tool and its craft profoundly affected—actually altered—society by changing the way we sat.

The turner's lathe is a relative of a household tool, the spinning wheel. A spinning wheel rotates a horizontal spindle that twists fiber into thread. A lathe rotates a horizontal spindle, usually the headstock, stuck firmly into one end of the piece of wood to be turned, called the "work." The other end of the work is passively held by the footstock's center pin, and when the headstock spins, so does the work.

The spinner's fingers reduced the fiber to the desired dimension; similarly, the turner's chisels reduced the spinning wood. Selecting from his assortment of sharp chisels, the turner held one, then another, to the rotating work, removing wood until the work was rounded, reduced to the desired breadth, and shaped to his design. A turner was most daring when he

continued to cut with the chisel deep into the wood, drastically thinning the wood; he was most skillful when he moved from a wide element to a narrow one in little space.

Ambitious sixteenth-century English turners left hardly an inch undecorated on their three-legged chairs. In their most audacious work, they cut the wood to create loose rings, completely free of the post. Soon they turned twisted, sometimes pierced, columns. Turners in seventeenth-century America did more modest work. Yet by then it was a mature craft, and theirs may have been turning at its most artistic (fig. 2.5). New Amsterdam (later New York) followed the similar turning tradition of the Dutch. Turners produced more chairs in colonial America than joiners and cabinetmakers combined.

Flamboyance, such as that seen in English sixteenth-century turnings, was common in a new craft and occurred because turning was then recently rediscovered. Like so much else, it had been dormant if not lost in the Dark Ages. The lathe had been known to the ancients, and turned furniture legs were a Roman favorite, yet no record remains of Roman lathes. Medieval Europe clearly didn't borrow Arabic, Persian, or Indian lathes, all of which required the turners to be floor-sitters. Chinese turners sat on seats and turned the work with treadle power, but Europeans did not know that. Their lathe required the turner to stand, usually resting his back against a rail.

Oddly, the English word "lathe" had no precedent in Europe.[4] Since the knowledge of the tool would have come from the Continent, this linguistic idiosyncrasy is probably a clue to the arrival of the tool in England. I think "lathe" derives from "lath," a rod or slat.[5] Apparently the first lathe that the English knew was the pole lathe, so called because it was powered by an overhead pole.

The horizontal pole held one end of a cord that was secured at the other end to a foot treadle. In between, the cord was wrapped round the work. A down stroke of the treadle flexed the pole. As it unflexed, it pulled on the cord, spinning the work. The action was reciprocal, not continuous as with the spinning wheel, modern lathes, or the "great wheel" lathe, which required additional manpower.

Turned work has now and again been fashionable, but never more so than when turned design was newly mastered. In early-

Figure 2.6. Flax spinning wheel, New England, 1700–1800. The design of the turnings remained persistent from the seventeenth century into the twentieth, when such wheels were still common in Appalachia.

sixteenth-century England, when pole-and-tread lathes were exciting new tools, treadle-driven flax wheels were too. Not incidentally, the new domestic devices were produced with the latest techniques (fig. 2.6).

Spinning wheels were omnipresent in colonial homes, someone was almost always spinning, and her occupation labeled the single woman "spinster." Flax wheels are good examples of the turner's art. The design of their turnings barely changed from the seventeenth century through the early nineteenth, when mills put home spinsters out of work except on poor rural farms.

Then, at the end of the nineteenth century, a Colonial Revival made "Pilgrim" turnings again fashionable. Flax wheels had the desired look, and those that had languished in American attics for generations were brought back downstairs as decorative objects. Some were taken apart and their turnings used to construct "antique" chairs. Home spinning was fondly remembered. but mostly the turnings just seemed so wonderfully "colonial."

The drop-spindle. the hand-spun top that twists and pulls the fibers as it falls from the hand and that Navajo women still use while tending their sheep. had little cachet as a colonial relic. The so-called great wheels. which required the spinster to stand (see a spinner at her great wheel. fig. 2.15). were rarely used decoratively. They took up more space and were either poorly turned or merely of stick construction.

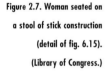

Stick construction. a primitive skill. yields furniture of round*ish* parts. such as those on the legs of the cook's stool (fig. 2.7). without using a lathe. A woodworker could use a branch much as it came from the tree. Commonly he split the wood. shaved the excess

away with a drawknife to form rounded sticks. and stuck them into (usually through) a plank forming a seat or tabletop. Common seats and tables in medieval Europe were stick. What furniture there was in American slave quarters was also likely to be stick. American Windsor chairs combined lathe-turned legs and stick construction: the so-called spindles of the back were sometimes merely whittled (fig. 2.8). The mortise joints on Windsors. like those on stick seats. often go through the plank.

Turners' chairs were assembled like joiners' chairs. They. too. were basically box frames. but the posts and rails were round. Like joiners' work. most turners' chairs used four posts (or legs). Turners. however. emulated stick construction by using rounded mortise-and-tenon joints instead of rectangular ones.

Turning flourished in the sixteenth and seventeenth centuries and dramatically changed the appearance of interiors. Turners made chairs and table bases. but they also supplied turned parts and embellishments for other furniture. even for joined case pieces. In the furniture trades. one craft often adopted the popular designs generated by another. Joiners incorporated turnings on the façades of their cases as decoration. even highlighting them by painting them black in imitation of ebony (fig. 2.9). Black turnings gleamed against the pale oak. Joiners responded to the competition of turners' chairs by acquiring lathes and turning parts of their chairs. Usually. the front posts of joined chairs—the most prominent legs—were partially turned. And a joiner who had no lathe might carve the posts

to impart a suggestion of turned work (see fig. 1.4c). The goal was to please the customer's eye, and in seventeenth-century America turned wood turned heads.

Turning remained popular in America. In New England, turned stretchers remained fashionable on eighteenth-century chairs that needed no stretchers and had no other turnings. Table legs that would be carved on an English or French example were turned on their American counterparts. Where Europeans put a simply turned column, Americans often put an elaborately turned post. Turning required less labor, and was therefore less expensive, than carving. In a nation without nobles and royals, it thrived as a popular way to decorate a shaft of wood and continued to charm.

Of even greater importance than the lathe's impact on decoration was its impact on chair productivity in the seventeenth century. The turner's art made chairs easily available, readily affordable, and increasingly popular—and at a time when people saw chairs as thrones for commoners. Those offered a chair in the seventeenth century were honored. A chair made one distinguished, hence "chairman," as in chairman of the board or committee chair. Using "chair" for a person is apt: "board" came from the table around which the members gathered under the oversight of the chair. (Similarly, the president's "cabinet" meets behind closed doors.) The man in the chair—it was usually a man—was the man of honor. Other men and most women sat on stools. Children did, too, if they didn't sit on backless benchs. Throughout the first century of American settlement, turners' chairs propelled a movement to chair-sitting, with its concomitant esteem.

Figure 2.8. Windsor armchair, maple, ash, oak, and pine. Southern Maine or coastal New Hampshire, 1775–1800. (Society for the Preservation of New England Antiquities.) The round legs come through the seat. A wedge driven into the end of each leg secures the joint.

Figure 2.9. Chest with two drawers, oak and pine. Blin workshop, Wethersfield, Connecticut, 1680–1700. (Historic Deerfield.) The case features carvings, applied moldings, and black-painted turnings.

SEX AND THE SINGLE CHAIR

Chairs are not gender neutral. The three favorite components of a parlor suite in the 1850s and the 1920s were sofa, "gent's chair," and "lady's chair." The gentleman's chair, always an armchair, was the most like a throne. The eclipse of ladies' and men's chairs is very recent, historically speaking. They lasted forty years into the twentieth century.

How did people read the gender of chairs? By breadth and arms. Wider seats were for men; status, not physique, ruled. To delete the arms or make them very low was to specify the distaff. In 1897 Mr. Sears catalogued armless rocking chairs as "Ladies' Rockers." A popular **fawbit:** "Hoop skirts like Scarlett O'Hara's brought about armless chairs." This theory was made out of whole cloth. Armless chairs for women are much older than Scarlett's skirts.

One form of chair now often termed a "slipper chair"—sold as a "sewing chair" in the 1860s and 1870s—was sexed by seat height. It might match a suite of chairs of standard height, except that its legs were shorter (fig. 2.10). A few such chairs were probably used by very short people, but in general they were for women. **Fawbit:** "Low chairs were designed to allow women to put on their slippers easily." Actually, mothers sat down low to reach young children. The lowdown is that men, too, wore slippers; they just didn't tend toddlers. The fawbit that supplied the name for the chairs is accurate only in recognizing them as women's chairs. Twentieth-century Americans could sit on the floor to tend a small child. Wearing jeans, it was easy. In Abigail Adams's day and attire, it was neither easy nor seemly. A low chair without arms allowed mothering arms free movement.

A low mother's seat had a European precedent surely known to the Pilgrims after their stay in Holland. Dutch women used a low basketwork or wickerwork birthing-nursing seat related to a cradle and called a *bakermat*.[6] The *bakermat* supported the mother's back and cradled her extended legs to her feet, creating from her lap a gently slanted swaddling place for the baby. The Dutch mother's wicker seat of the 1620s may be an ancestor of the low mother's chair in America.

The early colonists also used wickerware, but early wicker seldom survives. From paintings we know that basketwork chairs and cra-

Figure 2.11. *Portrait of George Wyllys,* oil on canvas, attributed to Joseph Steward, Hartford, 1785–1795. (Connecticut Historical Society.) Wyllys, once secretary of the colony, poses before his impressive bookcase, his legs straddling the center leg of his corner chair. He could write standing at his slant-lid desk (at right) or seated at his tripod table with its turned pillar base.

Figure 3.1. Horn armchair, original innerspring upholstery with jaguar-skin cover cloth, Wenzel Friedrich, ca. 1900. (The Witte Museum, San Antonio.)

William and Mary cane chairs and American banister backs affected the way turners ornamented the chair. They turned the back posts just above the seat simply, leaving them devoid of the fancy work they lavished elsewhere on the posts: the area would be hidden by a cushion on the seat. Similarly, they modestly turned the front legs just below the seat. The top of the front legs became merely backdrop for the tasseled ends of ties holding the seat cushion in place. The cushions, aptly referred to as "loose cushions," needed to be tied or they shifted on wood, cane, or rush seats. The design of the wood, therefore, reflected the impact of cloth—the cushion and tassels. That relationship would continue.

Even with cushions, sitting still on such chairs demanded physical endurance, for the erect, not quite vertical stance of the back forced a ramrod seating posture. To us, the chairs would not be comfortable. That, however, bespeaks our redefinition of the word. The Puritans found their chairs comfortable. *Comfort* meant "with strength," so the Puritan minister "comforting" the widow was dispensing fortitude, not ease. We gradually changed "comfort" to mean "ease," much as we changed what we demanded of our seats.

RESTING ON HORNS

Americans have relaxed on seats of many shapes, but probably among the strangest to our eyes are those that invite us to relax on horns (fig. 3.1). Horn furniture (steer horn was the favorite; elk and deer horn were also used) was at its most popular in the 1880s and 1890s, when upholstery was thriving and seating furniture had grown massive. Sturdy steer horns suited the new heftiness of chairs.

The chairs seem quintessentially masculine and evince the American West, yet they were not exclusively masculine and perhaps not so American. "American" horn chairs were produced primarily by German-Americans, who probably brought the idea from Germany: Wenzel Friedrich, a horn furniture manufacturer of San Antonio (working 1880–1890 or later); William Mittman, also of San Antonio (working 1881–1884); Charles Puppe, born in Prussia, who apparently took over Mittman's operation in 1885; and Herman F. Metz (working ca. 1890–1904) of St. Joseph, Missouri, who designed custom pieces. The Italian-American cabinetmaker Antonio Papeschi also worked with horn.

Friedrich produced steer horn tables, stands, and hat racks as well as seating, and Metz made case furniture with steer horn veneer and horns as handles. Horn chairs were made in Ohio and Chicago, then an important city for furniture production and, not incidentally, known for its stockyards. Hornware production was probably a sideline in several factories in the late nineteenth century, when German immigrants were prominent in the furniture trades.

Horn and antler seats with animal skin upholstery conjure up images of the Black Forest, Dürer's thick foliage, and the Grimm brothers' woods. In 1860 three antler chairs (of deer and elk antlers) sat in a ducal sitting room in Coburg among more usual parlor furnishings, a setting portrayed in a painting that Queen Victoria brought home from a visit to Germany.[1] In America, horn chairs would seem to have suited hunting lodges, men's libraries, and trophy rooms—rustic or masculine sanctuaries where animal heads routinely decorated the walls.

But animal heads and antlers also made their way into American parlors. Two tiger skins and a bearskin with its head lay on the marquetry floor in William H. Vanderbilt's drawing room on Fifth Avenue in New York, a room replete with piano, fringed chairs, and fringed and pillow-covered sofas.[2] Wherever animal heads belonged, so did horn chairs.

Upholstery enhances our impression of the chair's gender specificity. Animal skins were not the only choices. Friedrich's 1889 catalogue listed assorted skins as well as velvets—"plain or brocaded silk plush." Upholstered in velvet with long silk fringe as trim, the chair seems transformed, suitable for a woman and a parlor. Horn sofas, horn chairs with upholstered backs, and complete parlor suites of horn were available. A steer horn parlor suite finished in red velvet with a six-inch fringe may strike us as ideal for the sitting room of a brothel in Texas, yet not only brothel owners and Texans ordered them.

Tourists loved them. For Christmas 1888, Celia Gage Henderson received a horn chair from a cousin in San Antonio as a gift for her new home in cosmopolitan Cambridge, Massachusetts. There it remained until 1982, in a center of culture and learning.[3]

Clearly, a chair's show cover—velvet or

hide—was vital to its essence. Period documents from colonial times describe chairs by the material that covered them: "cane," "leather," or "green," the latter for the color of the fabric. It was the upholstery that caught the eye and the upholstery that distinguished one set of chairs from another to the upholsterer, the customer, and those taking an inventory. Equally vital to an upholstered chair was the stuff beneath the cover, the upholstery that made even a steer horn seat a place to rest.

UPHOLSTERER'S CHAIRS

Upholstery, the principal craft that made seats easy, arrived in mid-seventeenth-century America in the form of back stools. The radically new stuffed seats that we call Cromwellian—stools, back stools, and armchairs—provided the most luxurious and easiest seating of the time. The seat or back was an open wooden frame, covered with cloth by an upholsterer. His craft was to bridge the opening with straps, called "webbing" (fig. 3.2) and to cover them with a coarse fabric, which in turn supported the "stuff" (usually grass and a mere inch or so of hair). He then covered the stuffing with leather, the basic cover material, or

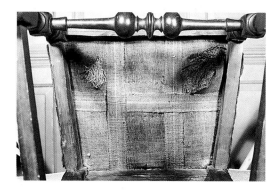

Figure 3.2. Underside of a chair (such as that in fig. 3.3c) with original upholstery. Three strips of webbing support the seat; straw stuffing is visible through holes in the bottom cloth.

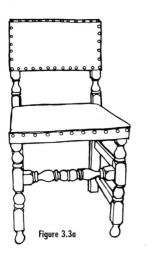

Figure 3.3a

Figure 3.3b

Figure 3.3c

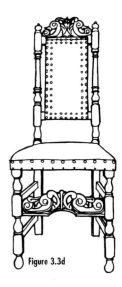

Figure 3.3d

plain wool or, if fancily done, embroidered cloth. The latter was often called "Turkey work," in honor of the Turkish carpet designs it imitated, but the English referred to the fancy cover cloths as "embroidered."

The expensive cloth covered much of the seat frame, although the base of the chair remained visible, often below a shallow fringe along the seat rail. The chair legs, and sometimes the front stretchers, were decoratively turned, occasionally quite elegantly. By the 1660s, the most prosperous Americans were lining the walls of their parlors and best rooms with such upholstered seating, a suite covered to match, hence the term "en suite." Armchairs were few; most seats were back stools and stools. Because few American cities provided enough work for an upholsterer, the suite was usually imported.

The elegant upholstered seventeenth-century chair seen in America's English and Dutch settlements and the simple wooden chair of the American Southwest (fig. 3.3b) were related. One chair was upholstered on the seat

and back; the other had wooden planks. The one was the work of a woodworker and upholsterer; the other the work of only a woodworker. The upholstered chair was the top of the line in its day; the joined nineteenth-century New Mexican chair, somewhat smaller and far more humble, never came near its classy competition. But they shared a common contour and a Spanish ancestor.

The dissemination of Spanish design followed trade routes and national flags. The southwestern chair took a direct path from Spain to Mexico, arriving with adventurers and clerics and staying put after part of Mexico became New Mexico. There, in an outback of Spanish design influence, the time-honored chair continued for centuries in basically the same simple form, small in size and all of wood. The exception is the twentieth-century "Santa Fe–style" chair that, although simply joined, might also be upholstered.

The upholstered chairs of New Amsterdam descended from Dutch chairs like those in Vermeer's paintings. Spain ruled the Nether-

Figure 3.3. Four side chairs: (a) back stool, wood and leather, Boston or New York, 1665–1695; (b) carpenter-made chair, wood, New Mexico, 1830–1930; (c) high back, wood and leather, Boston or New York, 1680–1710; (d) high back, wood and leather, Boston or New York, 1680–1715. Back stools could be ordered with matching low backs (a) and high backs (c). The low back (a) and the wooden chair (b) share the same basic shape and a Spanish tradition.

buy, for example, "chairs in the latest fashion," adding, "if the fashion be good." Their caution was understandable. With no Sears catalogue or Home Shopping Network, the British in America were ordering blind, and they were wary lest the design then being promoted in London circles be too extreme. Or too expensive. They usually gave agents a limit, such as, "The best to be had for £6."

Yet when buying an easy chair, an American looked to the closest city with an upholsterer and there placed the order. The upholsterer, who bought easy chair frames from a local cabinetmaker as he needed them, stocked the imported textiles needed as cover cloth, which he sold by the yard. He also had all the materials needed to put the ease in an easy chair: four pounds of curled hair and another four pounds of feathers. In rural areas, people might make an easy chair at home from

an old high-backed armchair, adding wings, padding, and coverings.

Although the American easy chair had precedents in seventeenth-century English invalids' seats and some homemade examples may have been invalids' chairs, by the middle of the eighteenth century, at least in America, upholsterers' easy chairs were not intended for invalids. Some have argued that eighteenth-century English easy chairs were solely for invalids, so those in America must have been as well. As evidence, they note that easy chairs were placed in bedchambers, which they were. But they also argue that easy chairs were usually pot-fitted, as were "chamber chairs" or "close stools," which in colonial America they were not. (In fig. 3.7, the seat frame was obviously not made for a pot.)

In colonial days, a corner chair (see fig. 2.11) was likely to be a close stool, not the upholsterers' easy chair. The invalid–easy chair theory equates the so-called wings with the nodding heads of sleepy septuagenarians. Wings blocked drafts (as did the wooden wings on settles), which proved useful for anyone in a drafty house. Easy chairs made after 1790 were more likely to be for the elderly and infirm and to be fitted for chamber pots. Such chairs were no longer high fashion, their heyday having passed because wings made easy chairs bulky, and the new neoclassical fashion called for a lighter look.

During the Federal era, prosperous merchants chose another kind of high-back chair, one upholstered over the entire back but without wings and open at the wooden arms (fig.

Figure 3.8. Young Lady with a Bird and Dog, John Singleton Copley (1738–1815), Boston, 1767. (Toledo Museum.) The height of fashion among the wealthy in 1767, lolling chairs became favorites in the Federal era.

3.8). Such chairs were another matter entirely. Called "lolling chairs" in their time, they later became widely known as "Martha Washington chairs." They were fashionable in parlors, often in pairs, whereas the easy chair had a history of being in a bedchamber and a single chair.

Able-bodied Americans enjoyed the ease of lolling chairs in their Federal parlors, much as their able-bodied forebears had taken to lolling in easy chairs in colonial bedchambers. Like the English attitude later toward the rocking chair, accepted at first only for invalids and nursing mothers, accepting easy chairs for the able-bodied was apparently harder for the English than for Americans. Yet prosperous colonials of middle years bought easy chairs primarily as a statement of success, perhaps having an eye toward maturity (as we might contribute to an IRA today). The chair was for the colonial well-to-do, the man who was successful, the woman no longer tending children, the sort of person who could afford yards of expensive cover cloth and the services of an upholsterer producing his most expensive chair.

The role of the easy chair in America is illustrated by the documented example seen here without its cover cloth (see fig. 3.7). Jonathan Sayward (1713–1797), a lumber merchant in York, Maine, bought the chair in 1759, seven years before he was elected to the Massachusetts legislature (Maine was then part of Massachusetts), thirteen years before he was named judge of probate, and at a time when his shipping business was very successful. His elderly mother had recently died, the house was at last his, and he and his wife were living alone, their only child having just married. They redecorated and added fashionable furniture and the easy chair—not a soft seat for any imagined infirm future but a sign of Sayward's fortune.

Although Sayward's green worsted easy chair was not made en suite with bed hangings and window curtains, some were. En suite or not, an easy chair went into a bedchamber with several other chairs, often a set of chairs. Through the third quarter of the eighteenth century, American bedchambers were sitting rooms where guests were welcome. Ensconced in the easy chair, the host or hostess held court.

The easy chair is but one instance of Americans adopting an English form and copying its location, yet modifying its use. In the late seventeenth century, they copied the English arrangement of table settings, placing a fork to the left of the plate. The English kept the fork in the left hand all the way to the lips while, an ocean away from the style setters, the colonials held the fork in the left hand only long enough to cut the food, then switched hands, bringing the food to the mouth with the right. The English way of eating is easier; our way with sitting was.

Sayward's chair is a rarity because we know its upholsterer, Samuel Grant of Boston. For upholstering it in green worsted, Grant charged £4:18:6, of which only 14 or 16 shillings went to the cabinetmaker for the frame. What Grant termed "Easie Cha'" was "Easie" because of all the stuffing. The expanse of green worsted said "ease." A sitter might even use a small footstool, often called a cricket. Ah,

ease. The path was set toward the overstuffed man's chair in the 1870s parlor and toward today's completely upholstered sofa and chairs.

EASIER STILL

The path also led directly to the recliner, the adjustable chair with a back that slanted down and a footrest that flipped up at the touch of a lever or a shift of the sitter's weight. Recliners owe something to English invalid chairs of the sixteenth and seventeenth centuries, but the chair that became sitting room furniture in the late twentieth century descended more directly from two others: the easy chair and a chair often associated with discomfort. On its way to becoming the modern recliner, the easy chair stopped off at the dentist's office.

Mechanical dental chairs, devised in the mid-nineteenth century, were aimed at making the patient's mouth readily accessible. Only very secondarily did they put the patient in such comfort as the situation could afford. At first American barber, dental, and surgical

Figure 3.9. Library of T. B. Winchester, Boston, 1890s. (Library of Congress.) The adjustable parlor chair beside the fireplace has a back that reclines and a footrest that can be elevated. The chair at the right, beside the library table, has an adjustable back; the chair at the left folds down to form library steps.

chairs were identical, for the same person was barber, dentist, and surgeon. By the 1890s, American barber's chairs reclined and revolved. In Europe, the barber chair remained a static and stiff seat into the 1940s: English barbers had to bend to look beneath their customers' chins, while American barbers merely tilted and turned customers. Efficient work was an American aim, and the chair was devised to suit the barber.

Surgeon-barber-dental chairs improved rapidly; many designs were patented and many models developed, bringing specialization. The dental chair came into its own with an adjustable back, headrest, and footrest—all the components of modern recliners—making it both easy chair and couch. By 1871 it had a parlor cousin. Or a library cousin (fig. 3.9). The 1890s photograph of the library of Mr. Winchester's Boston home shows a reclining parlor chair (in the center), a chair with an adjustable back (at the right), and a folding chair (at the left) that formed library steps.

G. Wilson, of New York, patented a cushioned iron-framed folding chair that sold in the tens of thousands. As illustrated in the catalogue of the Wilson Adjustable Chair Manufacturing Company, founded just to sell "the Wilson chair," the iron frame of the hybrid chair could be folded into six different pieces of furniture: a parlor chair, an easy chair with footrest, a lounge, a lounge with feet higher than the head, a child's crib, and an adult's bed.[5] The sitter accomplished this by simply folding three sections—the back, legrest, and footrest—by means of a lever. The arms reclined somewhat as the back lowered to a lounge. In the crib position the back remained upright and the arms stayed in place, forming partial sides. In the 1930s, I slept in my grandparents' parlor on a similar contraption. The ordinary-looking man's chair beside my grandparents' upright piano (which concealed no other furniture) folded into a crib.

STUFF AND SPRINGS

After mills and machinery took over textile production, the ready availability of inexpensive textiles had a huge impact on drapery and upholstery (fig. 3.10). Americans had barely covered the slip seats of their chairs in 1760; a century later they luxuriated in fabric. Exploding mill production generated what seemed unimaginable quantities of cloth, and upholstered backs and arms, once standard only on easy chairs, became standard on all parlor seats.

The combings of wool and short staple cotton generated as by-products in the textile mills were a boon to upholsterers. They substituted abundant wads of fluffy stuffing for the marsh grasses they had used earlier and generously augmented the thin layer of expensive animal hair. As upholsterers stuffed away, the nineteenth century saw parlor seats become softer, plumper, larger, and chair arms broaden into cylindrical bolsters. Many chair frames just about disappeared beneath cushions and mounds of softness (fig. 3.11). Often even the outline of the frame was lost.

Whereas eighteenth-century upholsterers had used rows of brass nails on over-upholstered chairseats to visually diminish the bulk. mid-nineteenth-century upholsterers emphasized cloth. sometimes leaving little more than the wooden feet of the chair showing. They added long fringe along the base of the seat. increasing the mass of textiles and sometimes hiding much of the chair leg. **Fawbit:** people put fringe on chairs and draped cloth over their pianos because prudish Victorians. thinking bare legs sexy. forbade bare wooden furniture legs in their parlors. They didn't confuse furniture with people; they had a passion for cloth. They heavily clothed parlor windows and hung portieres. fabric suspended in doorways in lieu of or in addition to doors.

By the 1860s. tufting—small buttoned-

Figure 3.10. Drawing room, decorated in Louis XIV style by Gustave Herter in 1860, Ruggles Morse house, Portland, Maine, 1893 photograph. (Victoria Mansion.) The man's chair (at the right) is wider than the ladies' chairs. Opulent drapery, imported carpet, and tufted and fringed upholstery make for a lavish parlor setting.

Figure 3.11. Drawing room, Fairman Rogers's new house, Newport, 1876. (Society for the Preservation of New England Antiquities.) The tufted and fringed ottoman and armchairs were the ideal of the time— softer, plumper, and larger parlor seats.

they tended to encourage a legs-up partly re- clined position, but two or more people could sit side by side, just as they had on long stools. Caned daybeds were popular at the start of the eighteenth century, when they took their place in American parlors as the principal bed moved from the parlor to the bedchamber.

During the colonial era, only a wealthy few bought upholstered multiple seats. Occasion- ally a prosperous colonist ordering a suite of chairs from a cabinetmaker included a match- ing two- or, very rarely, three-seat settee. Only the most prominent of colonists might order a sofa lushly upholstered over the arms and back. Because of the curves then in style, the upholstered back formed an undulating con- tour that was highest in the center. The form, completely upholstered except for its legs, came to be called a "camelback sofa." The term is a funny coincidence of words. What- ever ease the *suffah* gave the man on the camel's back, it did not approach the ease of sitting on a camelback sofa.

Colonists regarded a sofa much as they did an easy chair: as the ultimate in comfort. Though more than one person could sit on the sofa vertically, its upholstery also allowed—en- couraged—lounging. On top of the upholstered seat was a separate long feather-filled cushion, and against the rolled, upholstered arms and back might be added feather cushions, inviting the sitter to lean and relax. The recumbent posture was considered feminine, and the lady of the house was the one who might pose for her portrait on the sofa. Her position was sim- ilar to that assumed two centuries later by a "couch potato," a term that often suggested a man with a beer in his hand. When an eigh- teenth-century man sat on the sofa, he sat up- right beside his wife.

The colonists who sat on sofas were part of an exclusive set of wealthy, often urban, peo- ple. Other Americans regarded sofas and all that feathery softness as indulgences in com- fort, not suitable for themselves. Only after in- dependence did average citizens so indulge, first adopting the sofa, gradually taking to cushiness, and only in the mid-nineteenth cen- tury accepting a sofa as a parlor lounge.

As the nineteenth century began, Ameri- cans were looking back to ancient Rome, whose citizens were fond of lounging. Bernard Rudofsky entitled his fine history of manners and interiors *Now I Lay Me Down to Eat* be- cause Romans did just that. Their slaves ate while squatting on their haunches; free Ro- mans ate while reclining on couches, with cushions and bolsters at one end helping to keep their heads erect. Annually, Jews equate freedom with the Romans' dining pose: at the Passover Seder, a freedom feast, they celebrate by reclining while dining. Usually, a cushion added behind the sitter's back satisfies the need to lean.

The Americans of the young Republic, newly free, made the same connection between freedom and cushions and gradually adopted more and more cushions, although they sat on sofas feet down. During the Federal era, for the first time Americans seriously considered in- cluding a sofa among the usual assortment of parlor furniture. Lucy Hill was about to marry

Mrs CLARKE the York MAGNET.   See my Dol

when she selected her sofa (that in fig. 3.12). It did not match the parlor chairs she chose at the same time; this was often the case. If a family added only one thing to the parlor in the two decades after independence, it was a sofa. For a people anxious to emulate ancient Rome, using cushions and bolsters on sofas and couches was but one way. They, too, called their nation a "Republic" and borrowed Roman emblems like the eagle. Unlike the ancients, however, they sat erect in their dining rooms and on the sofas in their parlors.

Many Europeans were *"confortable"* on their *"fauteuils,"* including those who emulated the French, while many Americans continued to eschew lounging in their sitting rooms. An English visitor, Margaret Hunter Hall, noted in a letter in 1827 that people sat in "the American fashion as if they were pinned to the wall." She thought an American sofa was "a miserable, nasty, narrow thing with wood on which to break your elbows at every corner," and sofa bolsters were as "hard as logs of ebony."[8] She chose her simile well. Ebony, the hardest and blackest of wood, suggested the stiff black horsehair that was then the popular upholstery wood tears apart. Wood has compression strength; stretching breaks it. By 1840 Thonet had invented a technique of curving beechwood by bending metal and wood together. Soon he was producing amazingly tight and intricate bentwood curls and spirals (fig. 3.19). Thonet bent the steamed beechwood, round in cross section, by first clamping the wood to iron, then bending both together, with the iron on the outside forcing all the wood to compress. The firm developed a mass-production line in Vienna and they shipped the furniture in sections, to be assembled in ports of entry the world over.

Thonet's bentwood side chairs, combining light weight and grace, were especially popular in public places such as restaurants. A variation, bent wire chairs, became ubiquitous in ice cream parlors. By the late twentieth century, having garnered an aura of "antique," bentwood and bentwire chairs became popular in the casual rooms of the house, especially in kitchens (for ice cream parlor chairs, see fig. 5.11).

In the 1930s, when Americans were able to mass-manufacture tubular metal chairs of the cantilevered Breuer type far more cheaply than Europeans could, Americans relegated them to public places or kitchens. Perhaps in part because they were inexpensive. After the midcentury, however, tubular seating found a home in some American dining rooms but was rarely accorded a place in the parlor, where wood continued to be the material of choice.

Alvar Aalto (1898–1976), a Finn, was designing cantilevered parlor chairs of laminated wood by the 1930s. No wonder. Furniture makers and designers in the lumber-rich lands of northern Europe naturally thought in terms of wood. The floor runners on Aalto's chairs resembled skis for Finnish mountain slopes, curving upward into legs, arms, then backposts. Aalto steamed and curved his plywood cantilevered chairs much as Thonet had. A garden chair translated Aalto's continuous runner-leg-arm design into metal.

And so Europeans developed a series of twentieth-century cantilevered designs, all stemming from an idea planted by an American farm machinery designer who devised the cantilevered driver's seat on a tractor.

PLASTIC AND PLASTICITY

Twentieth-century Scandinavian designers thought wood; Bauhaus Germans thought metal; American designers thought plastic and pliable wood laminates. At a 1941 competition, the Museum of Modern Art awarded two first prizes, to Eero Saarinen (1910–1961) and Charles Eames (1907–1978), for their collaborative designs for chairs of laminated wood molded in three dimensions. Their three-dimensional approach was, in Saarinen's words, "a sculptural one, not the . . . constructivist one [of Europeans]."[13] The two men, architects and designers, met as students of Eero's father, Eliel, at Cranbrook in suburban Detroit. How appropriate! Where better than close by the Motor City to translate the American Windsor's sculpted wooden seat and the reaper's saddle-shaped metal seat into molded plywood chairs?

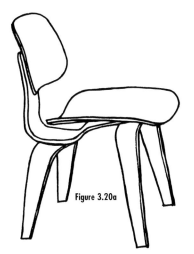

Figure 3.20a

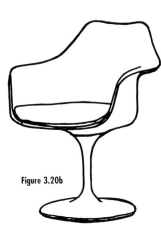

Figure 3.20b

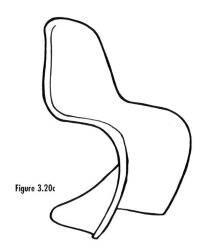

Figure 3.20c

Saarinen and Eames introduced molded plastic as a material for furniture, using it for the shells of chair seats. And they introduced resilient rubber-pad connectors between metal legs and molded plywood shells. The plywood and metal side chair that was designed in 1949 by Charles Eames and his wife, Ray (1916–1988), also a Cranbrook student, featured a seat and back of body-conforming wood laminate on thin metal legs. Another version stood on wooden legs (fig. 3.20a). Flexible rubber at the junctions allowed the chairback to yield to the individual sitter's own requirements. The chair's popularity stemmed in no small part from its give and body-sympathetic configuration. The Eameses' lightweight chair followed in the tradition of the readily portable seat once filled by Windsors and later by Thonet's bentwood chairs.

Eero Saarinen shaped plastic much as the Eameses shaped plywood. His 1948 upholstered chair, known as the "womb chair," had a shape similar to that of the Eames chair. His 1955 tulip suite—side chair, armchair (fig. 3.20b), and table (see fig. 5.11)—was grace on a pedestal. It seemed to owe something of its simplicity and sinuous line to a Georgia O'Keeffe painting of a Jack-in-the-pulpit. It also owed something to Thonet's chairs and to the swiveling desk chair on a pedestal. Saarinen prided himself that his pedestals freed a room of "a slum of legs."[14]

Saarinen's molded plastic tulip chairs had their own descendants, all molded in one piece. One chair (fig. 3.20c), designed for Herman Miller in 1960 by Verner Panton, a Swiss, was expensive, and when it appeared in *American Home* in May 1968, it was not yet available in America. Other molded plastic chairs cost so little that they bloomed worldwide on garden patios, lawns, and porches in the 1990s.

The inexpensive chairs, selling from stacks piled up wherever housewares are sold, look body-sympathetic, but they vary incredibly. Some are comfortable, some are handsome, some are sturdy, some are none of the above. They present intriguing possibilities. Since sitters vary in their proportions, might molded

Figure 3.20. Side chairs: (a) plywood and rubber, designers Charles and Ray Eames, U.S.A., 1946; (b) "tulip" side chair, molded plastic, designer Eero Saarinen, U.S.A., 1955; (c) stackable side chair, molded plastic with glass fiber, designer Verner Panton (b. 1926), Switzerland, 1960. Chairs (a) and (c) manufactured by Herman Miller, (b) by Knoll.

plastic chairs—already available in several colors—be made in many sizes and sold like off-the-rack clothing?

What the best plastic chairs—Saarinen's, Panton's, and some others—did was conform with a popular twentieth-century design ideal, the fluid line. For much of the century, design around the house was flowing: kidney-shaped backyard pools, the undulating tops of Isamu Noguchi's tables, Alexander Calder's mobiles, Eero Saarinen's tulip suite, and Dale Chihuly's vases. The line had meandered in from Art Nouveau. It shaped George Ohr's vases in the first decade of the century and Hans Arp's sculpture in the next; it confronted classicism and post-and-beam and dominated midcentury design with a soft curve, extolled at the time as "plasticity," "fluidity," "biomorphism," "organic," "free-form," and "fluid contours."

The impetus for plasticity in the twentieth century was the effort to design forms that appeared sympathetic to the human body. One way to accommodate people of various sizes is with a chair that reshapes itself for each sitter. The introduction of inflatables by Italian designers in 1967 aimed to do just that. Inflatable

Figure 3.21. Beanbag, blue, red, black, and green denim bag, embroidered ABC, filled with eps foam beans. Produced by Easy Bean, San Francisco, 1990s.

seating was wonderfully inexpensive if not wonderfully durable. One PVC (polyvinyl chloride) inflatable designed in 1967, the Quasar, was a sort of tire tube of a chair that sold for $12.95. In 1969 a clear plastic square hassock—a round hole in the center made it look like a tire with corners—sold for $4.95 when the magazine illustrating it, *Decorating Your First Home*, sold for $1.35.[15]

The beanbag chair (fig. 3.21) quickly followed inflatables. The soft and yielding seat, a plastic sack filled with polystyrene pellets, was far less rigid than the air-filled inflatables: it was all plasticity. Mass-produced and inexpensive, the chair took its shape from the sitter's body. That's organic. Much upholstery in the late twentieth century aimed at conforming to the sitter's shape by remaking its own contours.

Americans had flirted with sitting on the floor, using floor cushions and lowering tables to suit. We were emulating the Japanese, just as they were emulating us by sitting on chairs. Chair-sitting took hold there; floor-sitting here did not. We tried sitting, feet down, on bancs built into the floor, called "conversation pits." Like castle window bancs, only the cushions were movable. Inflatables and beanbag chairs may have been the culmination of American floor-cushion-sitting. By 1980 cushions had risen to sofas and beds. There they ended a period of cushionless sofas and flat and tightly upholstered parlor seating. In the 1980s and 1990s, Americans enjoyed much softer upholstered seats than they had at midcentury. The emphasis was on cushions and pillows, fluff that conformed to each sitter.

The same 1969 issue of *Decorating Your First Home* showed suites of cutout seating, called "modular" (the term sounded modern), looking like so many jigsaw pieces blown up to the size of furniture. One suite, designed "strictly for the young at heart," was "stackable, pack-up-and-go, polyurethane foam . . . covered in a sleek, jersey-like stretch fabric."[10] The "basic ottoman" was $79. Modular units were touted as easily rearranged or moved to the next domicile. The "jersey-like stretch fabric" barely outlasted relocation, and the bulk of the modules inhibited easy rearrangement in any but large spaces. Jigsawed modular seats, corner seats, and ottomans worked better in airport terminals than in homes.

By 1972 the architect and designer Frank Gehry (b. 1929) added to jigsawed seating several graceful cutouts of corrugated cardboard, named "Easy Edges" for the soft fabric-like texture of the cut surfaces. Easy Edges, like the "jersey-like" covers on the polyurethane cutouts, hinted at upholstery while offering none of the elegance associated with upholstered goods. The cutouts had flowing lines but formed rigid and unyielding seats.

CURVES, HORNS, AND ANCIENT GREEKS

All that plasticity had an early-nineteenth-century wooden ancestor, made in America but based on Greek design. In 1808 Samuel Gragg (1772–1855) of Boston patented a chair of solid woods—oak, beech, maple, birch, and ash (fig. 3.22). He bent the oak and beech using heat, water, and molds and made the

wood run from the top of the back along the seat down to the foot in a graceful, flowing line. The curve, from back to seat to leg, was plasticity itself. The wood of the back seemed to yield like suspended cloth that takes its shape from the sitter's body. No wonder Gragg dubbed his bentwood chair "elastic."

The Eameses' birch plywood chair (see fig. 3.20a), a sort of extraterrestrial quadruped that just happens to support human bodies ideally, began to evolve in 1808 when Gragg bent wood to better fit the body. Thonet tightened the bentwood curves and, through mass production, spread the fluid line worldwide. Then technology enabled manufacturers to mold plywood and plastic.

The perception of comfort and actual comfort, however, are two different things.

Figure 3.22. Side chair, oak and beech (bent elements), maple (round stretchers), birch (front seat rail), ash (rear seat rail); H: 34⅜"; W: 18⅛"; D: 25⅜". Samuel Gragg, Boston, 1808–1815. (Winterthur Museum.) Gragg patented his process for making bent chairs.

Americans borrowed from Victorian England the richly ornamented "Picturesque" style, with its irregular and asymmetrical façades, they altered the building design by adding the porch. Britons followed—not at all the usual direction of Anglo-American design—adding porches to their Picturesque houses.

Not that the English could not already enjoy the views of their gardens. Large eighteenth-century British houses had rear terraces, elevated above the ground, onto which one could step directly from a room and descend to the garden. Terraces had masonry floors, as the name suggests, but no roofs. Such British estates might also have a gazebo or folly, a small, discrete, roofed structure often built in an exotic style, from which to enjoy the gardens. Set out amid the greenery, gazebos were the purview of the privileged. Only when the English began attaching porches to their houses could ordinary Englishmen sit outside under a roof.

Americans relished living out of doors yet at home (figs. 4.7, 4.8). They used, furnished, and equipped their porches in various ways. In 1896 in his "front porch campaign" (see fig. 2.20), William McKinley actually ran for president while he appeared to be relaxing at home and inviting the nation to his doorstep. The Johnsons, sitting on their porch, had just fin-

Figure 4.7. Biggs house porch, undated print. (Cincinnati Historical Society.) The porch has a hammock, ladderback rocking chairs, an iron railing, and a trellis. Porches frequently had trellises overgrown with vines.

Figure 4.8. Mother and children on their screened porch, September 1913. (State Historical Society of Wisconsin.) A pillow-covered porch swing hangs in the background.

ished campaigning (see fig. 3.14). For the spinner (see fig. 2.15), the porch was her work and living space. For many like her, much of living was working. For others, porches were primarily for relaxation and casual socializing.

Although roofed, many porches were also equipped with shades or awnings. Some, especially during the early twentieth century, had screens (fig. 4.8). Nineteenth-century porches occasionally had Venetian blinds; others had elaborately rigged shades of canvas or reeds. Porch shades were popular with all except those who had to hang them every spring, with all their cords and pulleys. People used the shades as sunscreens, not privacy screens.

Passersby saw porch-sitters; their screens were not the equivalent of English garden walls and hedgerows, keeping eyes out. Robert Sutcliff readily observed Philadelphians sitting on their porches in full view in 1806. "These piazzas are commonly six feet wide with boarded floors. On seeing families seated in them in their tranquil summer evenings, it constantly reminded me of the patriarchs of old, sitting at the doors of their tents in the cool of the day."[3]

THE PUZZLE

Because the porch became part of American house design before being adopted in style-setting Europe, one can pose the question, "How did Americans come to this attached outdoor room?" Might one individual, some unknown American Palladio, have turned the palazzo inside out?

known in the traders' homeland because they never saw what the slaves built. The porch thrived in the amalgam that was American culture, and after Americans altered some nineteenth-century English house designs to add porches, the English took note, liked what they saw, and attached the American porch to their Victorian homes.

Porches flourished through the 1800s. They were especially popular in the rural South, where the front porch proved ideal for churning butter and weaving cloth and as the year-round toilet place for a morning's wash and shave (see pages 182–183). Ironically, most slave quarters had no porches except for one on the nursery, where very young children stayed while their mothers worked in the field. (The inside story of slave cabins is on pages 181–182.)

Another irony, and another transatlantic journey. In the mid-nineteenth century, the freed slaves who went back to Africa took the porch with them to West Africa, whence it had not come. Monrovia, Liberia, got red brick houses with wide verandahs.

UP FRONT AND PUBLIC

For most of its American history, the porch was at the front door to greet people. Having arrived as a surrounding porch, it proliferated in the late eighteenth and early nineteenth centuries, often as a front porch, thanks to the portico. It flourished in the late nineteenth century often as a surrounding or almost surrounding porch, and as the twentieth century began it still enveloped the front door.

The nineteenth-century porch was open and all-inclusive. In an era when children might be forbidden access to some rooms (the parlor) and women to others (a man's study or billiard room), all ages and both sexes were welcome on the casual porch. As one sat and rocked, as two sat on a porch swing (like the Johnsons, fig. 3.14), or as families chatted in small clusters, neighbors walked by within view, often within earshot. Greetings were commonly exchanged. Sometimes how-dos led to an invitation to the porch. With lightweight, casual seats, porch groups easily reclustered. The steps also served as seats.

Stoop-sitting in the city was like front porch–sitting. The stoop of a four-family urban brownstone was a sort of communal porch; the individual house porch was family turf, open to the community. Both were places for family conversations, neighborly talk, and lemonade. Or tea. In June 1806, Robert Sutcliff "found the family sitting in the shade of the piazza, in front of the house, where we joined them in taking tea and enjoyed the freshness of the breeze, and a beautiful prospect of a part of the country between his house and Philadelphia."[14]

Anyone coming to the house was first scrutinized by those on the porch and could be delayed there or deterred from entering. The nineteenth-century porch was a front front parlor, largely devoid of display, completely devoid of pomp, but rich in homeyness. Although the porch was not cluttered with grand possessions like the parlor was, nineteenth-century architecture was highly decorative, extensively ornamented, and much of it surrounded the porch. Architectural details thrived in an era when people walked by at a leisurely pace.

SIDE PORCHES

Then the porch shifted to the side of the house, and the decorative detailing diminished. Since the porch had no direct access to the street, those sitting on the porch, while still in view of street and sidewalk, were decidedly removed from passersby. Some remoteness—certainly not privacy—had been bought at the price of some removal from the action. Having meandered to the side, the porch stopped there only for a while.

The side porch of the 1920s–1940s—often screened, sometimes enclosed by glass—extended neither around the front nor to the back. Many houses had side porches up and side porches down that were entered only through the house. Sleeping porches on upper floors (fig. 4.12), usually entered through a bedroom, were at the side, often directly above a sitting porch, or in the back. A large house

Figure 4.12. Gamble House, Greene and Greene architects, Pasadena, California, 1908. (Gamble House.) Upstairs porch at right is a boy's sleeping porch.

might have more than one sleeping porch—a second-story one for the boys, one on the third story for the girls.

In 1908, Charles Sumner Greene and Henry Mather Greene designed the Gamble house in Pasadena, California, as a winter vacation home for the Gambles of Procter &, featuring second-story porches overhanging sitting porches. This spacious house and its ilk were modestly called "bungalows." The word, which like "verandah" carried connotations of India, specified a house whose spreading roof covered a porch, and a fashion for bungalows followed.

For their second home, the Gambles stinted on nothing—not size, not cost—yet the bedroom for their two sons was only large enough for dressing. It could not hold two beds. The boys, home on vacation from boarding school, slept on their own sleeping porch off their bedroom, one of three such second-story porches.

Before air conditioning, sleeping in the cool desert air was ideal. Eighteenth-century Americans had eschewed fresh night air and deemed it unhealthful; a century later Americans sought it out. Fearful about tuberculosis, they generally believed it was healthy to sleep outdoors. Yet sleeping porches were always more than just healthy outdoor bedchambers. To adults they were also private sitting rooms; to children they were casual, festive sleeping places, rather like camping out in a tent.

During the twentieth century, many side porches were built with screening, many older front porches had screens added, and many of both were enclosed with glass. In rural areas,

on very modest homes, the old open porches remained in use, but in towns and cities most were enclosed as rooms or demolished. America's streets would be lined with many more front and side porches had they not been "renovated" out of existence. So many had disappeared that in 1967 the magazine *American Home* could use the headline "Remember Screened Porches?" to announce their return. The returning porch they envisioned, however, was at the rear of the house.

REAR PORCHES

Changes in the location of the porch did not change its casual nature. Its furniture, still designed for relaxation, might include rocking chairs and gliders. But the nature of relaxed living changed because placement affects the way a room is used. The change began early in the twentieth century when the several porches on houses such as the Gambles' created individual, private places. The sleeping porch off the boys' room was for the boys; that off an adult's bedroom, for that adult. When the family porch moved to the rear, it separated the family from its neighbors, creating a very different setting from that enjoyed by front porch–sitters.

In 1967, three months before *American Home* promoted the return of screened porches, it featured a suburban New Jersey house designed by Richard Meier. The façade was two long, windowless brick walls, with a landscaped mound of earth obscuring much of the entry. Meier's aggressively protective façade was the opposite of the welcoming openness of a front porch. The large windows and glass doors of the house looked out to the rear.

Since the mid-twentieth century, the family's outdoor space has usually been behind the house, be it patio, deck, screened porch, conservatory, or simply a fenced or plant-screened backyard. A twentieth-century back porch is no relative of a back porch a century earlier. That sometimes discrete small porch, a kitchen or service porch, was a place for homely tasks such as cleaning the chicken of its feathers. Sometimes the rear of the encircling porch was similarly used (note the maid at the left, fig. 4.1).

More recent rear porches, like the old front sitting porches, were designed for open-air family relaxation but were not to be seen from the street. With its relocation, the porch became an inner sanctum that callers might never reach. In a complete reversal of the nineteenth-century relationship between porch and house, the house protected the porch.

The private porch grew so important to twentieth-century Americans that apartment dwellers demanded its equivalent. The era of the rear-facing porch became the era of the apartment's outdoor room, the "terrace" or "balcony." Continuing a practice common with side porches, some apartment dwellers—perhaps those who came from the side porch tradition—enclosed their porches with glass. Others chose open spaces, screened or not.

The furniture for apartment porches, the usual bamboo or pseudo bamboo, wicker, rattan, metal, or plastic, sat on floors worth noting. Because the base was concrete, traditional wooden porch floors were virtually precluded. Floors open to the weather might be ceramic, suggesting the garden terrace albeit with a roof, or painted, usually green, or covered with indoor-outdoor carpet, invariably green. Green reads as "grass" and "garden."

Simulating with color has been established porch practice. Nineteenth-century wooden porch floors were painted gray, not green. At that time, cobblestone streets and slate walks, both gray, were welcome improvements on rutted dirt roads, alternately dusty or muddy, so gray porch floors read very well. Porch ceilings were painted azure blue. The blue **fawbit:** "Blue paint was standard on porch ceilings because blue repels insects." If so, it would have worked better closer to the people—on the furniture or the floor. Actually, blue suggested the sky. Sky blue up, stone gray or lawn green down, the painted message of porches and apartment terraces reads "outdoors."

PERIPATETIC FOR CAUSE

The porch has been peripatetic because Americans are. Its twentieth-century travel around the house was a reaction to the automobile. When the Oldsmobile went into volume production in 1902, people were enjoying seeing their neighbors walk by and strangers pass. In the 1920s, when Americans were taking to the mechanized car, those on porches found it less appealing to watch neighbors drive away or strangers speed by.

The motor car pushed the porch from its place encompassing the front door. At first it went to the side of the house but merely paused there. The explosion in automobile production after World War II filled the streets with engine noise, exhaust odors, and sedan-enclosed passersby. Fewer people walked by. In 1961 Jane Jacobs, in *The Death and Life of Great American Cities*, saw the essence of city life coming from people's interest in watching people.

Jacobs said that people, by watching the streets, made them safer. Some people say the porch's retreat to the back was a consequence of unsafe streets. It's just the opposite. First came the cars, then the pedestrians diminished, then the street became less safe and less friendly.

The automobile also encouraged movement out of the city to green spaces—to garden towns and suburbia—which stemmed from the idea "green is good." Pavement and city streets—the once-beneficial gray—were equated with "bad." Community planners, as Vincent Scully says, came "to loathe the density of the city and to hate its streets."[15] That was not good news for front porches.

Radburn, a planned community (1928) in Fair Lawn, New Jersey, separated its coveted green space from the street. Built for railroad commuters (sited on a train line), it provided for a family's owning one car. Most important, the design removed the inviting open spaces—shared commons with quiet walkways amid greenery—from cars and the street, hiding the green behind the houses.

After 1950 suburbs proliferated; most commuters drove to work. Suburban families often had two cars but a garage for only one. In the 1990s, they often needed three. Suburbanites in 1950s houses with one-car garages and one-car driveways turned more and more to parking on the street, and parked cars joined the views of green front lawns. Radburn's residents, increasingly cramped for car space, were lucky, however. Their green space already shunned the street.

Some exurban subdivisions fostered the illusion of removal from the street by erecting estate-like entrances displaying estate-like names: Pheasant Brook, Fox Run, Rabbit Ridge. The names invoked nature, although the "Brook" was probably in a culvert, not a "Pheasant" or "Fox" remained, and what would "Run" were rabbits and cars. Some subdivisions promised safety by gating the community—the epitome of street hostility. Safe within the gates, porches were still in the rear, still avoiding the street.

Mindful of the street, both garage and porch have moved in sympathy to each other. At first the car went into the carriage house, which, as shelter for the horse as well as the carriage, was set apart from the house. At first, garages, like earlier stables and carriage houses, provided automobiles with houses of their own, sometimes with rooms for the chauffeurs. The "detached" garage was misnamed: no one detached it; it started out on its own.

After World War II, people wanted a room for the car instead of a separate building behind the house. Since no horse was there, a room within the house was possible. Why walk outdoors in foul weather or carry groceries farther than necessary? The mistress of the house was now carrying the groceries; the question would not have come up if a staff still did the toting. The garage—or its cheaper version, the carport, a roofed parking space—was attached at the side of the house. This cleared the grounds to the rear, ending an age-old tradition of outbuildings, often out back.

The backyard, cleared of the stable/carriage-house/detached garage, was free to become the family's green space. In 1987 the *New York Times* touted the backyard as "A New Room in the House."[10] The accompanying illustration depicted swings, kiddie pool, barbecue, umbrella-shaded table and chairs, lounges for sunning and reading. Not a porch in sight. In the 1980s, some people were still removing their old front and side porches or enclosing them as family rooms, believing that air conditioning precluded the need for porches. But other homeowners started to roof the backyard terrace or to augment the sunny rear deck with a porch. Some attached small porches behind attached garages. With the rear vista open after the garage's removal, rear porches thrived. Large glassed expanses looked to the back, and the open view from the porch became integral to the house itself.

Almost in lockstep with the porch moving rearward, the garage moved forward. By the 1990s, it had become an architect's biggest challenge. At almost a 24-foot square for a two-car garage, a 36- by 24-foot block for three cars, the room for the cars was usually the biggest room in the house. Thrusting such an ungainly bulk forward dramatically affected, and often hid, the front of the house. The front was not where the action was. The action, like the porch, was in the rear.

PUTTING THE PORCH
IN ITS PLACES

While all porches are open, some have always seemed more open than others because of their placement or design. A porch that was merely a step above the ground needed no railings and allowed entry all along its periphery. That's open. A somewhat higher porch floor, perhaps because of a basement, required railings and consequently imparted some sense of enclosure. Shotgun porches seldom had railings. Many rural porches had none; some homeowners couldn't afford them. Others did not want them. On July 4, 1996, the *New York Times* quoted a woman in South Carolina who saw railings as less than welcoming. Her "open porch," she felt, invited people to "stop and talk, and that's a friendly kind of feeling."

Upper-story porches needed railings. Just by being higher, they were more private. Jean de Pradel's three hundred feet of second-story gallery around his grand 1753 house would have seemed more removed than the three hundred feet of gallery below. On many plantation houses, only the upper porch had railings; the lower level was on the ground, accessible all around. On a large, secluded plantation, however, even such a lower porch was a private place.

The people of Charleston, South Carolina, long ago removed their porches from the street; since the 1740s, their single or tiered double porches have faced their private side gardens. The main façade of the house, with its entrance door, does too. The typical Charleston house (fig. 4.13) presents a narrow

nation of porch-sitters had come to expect grand vistas, but whatever the reason, the nation proved a ready market for imported scenic wallpapers and painted murals.

Small figures often peopled wallpaper landscapes, and Americans were apt, at least in inns, to make cartoons out of such scenes. In the 1830s Harriet Martineau, the English traveler, found that parlor walls in inns seemed "to be an irresistible temptation to idle visitors . . . to put speeches into the mouths of the painted personages; and such hangings are . . . deformed with . . . American witticisms put into the mouths of Neapolitan fishermen, ancient English ladies of quality, or of tritons and dryads." [2] An earlier example of balloon speech is the circa 1760 drawing done by a guest at the Charleston home of Harriet Manigault's grandfather, Peter Manigault (1731–1773), then Speaker of the Carolina Assembly (fig. 5.2).

By the mid-nineteenth century, framed landscapes were popular. The paintings, often surprisingly large, opened wondrous scenes before those comfortably seated on upholstered parlor suites. The vistas in American landscape paintings seem far broader, less hemmed in at the sides, than their European counterparts. Only Dutch landscapes, with their low horizons, seem similarly open. The expansiveness of American landscapes owes much to the countryside itself, to the New World of immense spaces. But customers, too, affect fashion, and the people who bought a Thomas Doughty, Asher Durand, Fitz Hugh Lane, John Frederick Kensett, or Frederic Church—or a work by many another painter—obviously wanted wide, if framed, vistas. Accustomed as they were to viewing a bit of the natural world from their porches, Americans chose large landscape paintings for their parlors, giving their formal sitting rooms some of the openness of their casual sitting places.

Nineteenth-century builders also increased indoor visibility. They opened spaces by using wider doorways, double doorways, and enlarged windows, made possible by improvements in glass production. Each new style brought larger windows and larger individual panes. The resulting interiors, lit by daylight, encouraged more artificial light after dark. Indoor living changed dramatically, and it all began with a hole in the wall.

WINDOWS

At the time of the European settlements in America, a dearth of fresh air—let alone a lack of a view and little illumination—typified all the houses. The stifling, dark interiors of early colonial dwellings were rather like those of mankind's rudest shelters and very like those in medieval Europe, when the interiors of castles and hovels alike were dark, cramped, and almost airless. Airless and malodorous at once. Most of the air in a primitive dwelling came through a hole in the roof that allowed the

smoke of the fire to escape. Light came in the way smoke left.

Originally the castle hearthstone was set in the center of the vast hall or main room, and the smoke hole was in the center of the roof. Later, the hearth was moved up against a wall. No chimney yet. In Tudor England, a house with its hearth against the wall had a smoke hole at the apex of the gable, replacing the hole in the center of the roof. It was a smoky solution, smokier than the one the Plains Indians devised when shaping the entire tepee to form a chimney.

Then someone built a chute above the hearth for the fire's smoke, the chimney, widely adopted by the English in the sixteenth century. That improved the air indoors no little bit. But in order to get air into the room—air was needed or the fire could not burn—one needed a hole in the wall. In addition, a hole in

Figure 5.2. Drawing, ink and wash on paper, George Roupell, Charleston, South Carolina, 1760. (Winterthur Museum.) Roupell was one of the guests enjoying drinks at the home of Harriet Manigault's grandfather, Peter. The multipaned window is bare of curtains. The talk—"Whose Tost is it?"—bores the slave on the right, but the parrot by the window may learn a word or two from the man, his back to the fireplace, who toasts, "Success to Caroline, G—d dame."

bed." He asked, " 'Who's there?' and was answered by a girl, who was burrowing for eggs; part of the stores . . . kept in boxes, in this convenient locality."[4]

Near the end of the seventeenth century, houses of the "better sort" had fireplaces in upstairs bedchambers and food storage elsewhere. Heated eighteenth-century chambers were used very like downstairs parlors, as sleeping-washing-eating-birthing-courting-dying-sitting rooms. Downstairs, the hall and parlor still had beds; upstairs, a chamber had as many chairs as the parlor or the hall. When Captain Ruggles died in 1716, he had thirteen chairs in his "Parler," fifteen in "the Hall," and fifteen in his bedroom, named for its location above the parlor "the Parler Chamber."[5] Meals often were taken upstairs, and guests routinely were received there. With guests ascending the stairs, the nature of the stairway changed and the entry became an entirely different place.

THE GLORIOUS EIGHTEENTH

Enter a new hallway, a new era, and a genteel fashion called "Georgian" for George I, II, and III, our rulers from 1714 to independence. A new gentility pervaded the eighteenth century and dominated the entry or staircase hall. Everything was formal. Since the rest of the interior was formal as well, the gracious entry delivered what it promised.

The Georgian era brought classical ornament to America. The newly arrived officials of the Crown who introduced the fashion had a taste for English formality, London modernity, and more consumer goods. Symmetry, a great

novelty of the new architecture, established a major difference between American houses built before 1700 and those built afterward. The new architecture featured classical pediments, columns, and pilasters. White paint, contrary to popular belief, was not essential to the Georgian look. Pseudo-marble white houses dominated the landscape only after the Revolution.

The most dramatic Georgian change to the house was to its entry hall. Placed at the center of the house, it was also at the center of activity. It ran from the front through to the back of the house, affording access to all the rooms, and its stairway presented the path to the rest. The hall introduced the entire interior.

The new house plan spurred the segregation of functions that had begun so modestly in that rear service room across the back of seventeenth-century saltboxes. The hall was the divider of spaces while it, itself, was a place apart. Wallpaper was very popular in the eighteenth century, and certain patterns thought appropriate for "entry," "hall," or "staircase." Distinct from other wallpapers, these tended to have large designs, thereby enhancing the hall's separateness and additionally distinguishing the adjoining rooms from one another.

Yet the formal, genteel, center hall held the Georgian house together. The Royall House, in Medford, Massachusetts, originally built of brick in 1690, was enlarged in 1732–1739 in the new fashion. Its impressive hallway (fig. 6.3) dates from the 1730s. The house exemplifies the change brought by the new style and illustrates the important unifying role of the

central hall, which runs through the house from one centered door to another.

The house has two thresholds, two façades. One faces the road, the other the river. In the 1700s, distant travelers and most merchandise arrived by water. Many a Georgian house with a through central hall faced two ways at once. Whichever threshold was crossed, the hall led to all four rooms on the main floor, two on each side. Such stylish Georgian houses might be few, perhaps one or two in a community—Royall's was unique in Medford, where other houses were in the old saltbox style—but a town's Georgian building defined what was fashionable.

While in the South the kitchen often stood removed from these four rooms—off to the side toward the front or in the rear—in the North, it was one of the two back rooms and defined the rear of the house. When New Englanders first took cooking out of the hall, in about 1690, they moved it into a lean-to running along the back of the saltbox house. Placing the service area at the less publicly accessible rear made sense; access to the garden and field was also important. Also, the lean-to's long roofline lessened exposure to the weather, a decided advantage if it was placed to meet the north wind. Putting cooking chores, with the heat they generated, in a north room also made sense. So in

Figure 6.3. Entry hall, Isaac Royall House, Medford, Massachusetts, 1730s. (Royall House Association.) A grand staircase awaits just beyond the arch that frames this through hall. One exterior door is behind the camera; another, straight ahead.

thereby forming a perfect protection to the upholstery and carpet."[28] A separate bathroom was a great convenience.

Until it was built in, however, little had changed since 1438, when Saint Barbara was depicted with a ewer and basin for washing in her room (see fig. 1.6). People washed up and shaved on the porch of many a southern house year-round (see fig. 7.14; a washstand is at the left). The omnipresent gourds on southern porches were part drinking vessel and part toiletry equipment. While in the countryside the only place to wash up might be at the kitchen sink, bedroom toilet sets were common in cities and among the well-to-do. In 1897 Sears offered five crockery sets, from eight to a dozen matched pieces, including a basin and large pitcher; a mug, brush holder, and small pitcher; a covered soap dish with drainer; covered slop bowl, and covered chamber pot. Sears's decorated sets (the cheapest was plain white) depicted flowers; two were named Azalea and Chrysanthemum. Vendors shrewdly chose appealing names for toilet and bath.

Near the end of the nineteenth century, the bathroom developed as a single room, a bathing-washing-toilet closet off or near the bedroom or bedrooms. It replaced the outdoor privy, the washstand with toilet set in the bedroom, the gourd on the porch, and the tub in the kitchen. From the first, the American bathroom was unified, not the separate water closet and bathroom of Continental fashion. Americans knew of bidets, but few owned them in the days before plumbing or adopted them as a standard fixture.

So the bathroom began as a convenience, indoors and clean. Its most esteemed attributes can be read in the design names used by plumbing suppliers. J. L. Mott's 1888 catalogue of plumbing fixtures—277 pages with 844 illustrations, 40 in color—offered water closets named Inodoro (perhaps a wordplay on "indoor"), Purita, Hygeia, and Dolphin, whose hopper was shaped like one.[29] It also featured porcelain and porcelain-lined bathtubs called "Roman Baths" and "French Baths." The "French" had one sloped end as backrest, emulating a chaise longue in a boudoir (like that in fig. 6.13). The "Roman" had the faucet centered on one long side, allowing for two sloped ends, apparently for two bathers. Its name acknowledges that Roman bathing was not an activity for one person.

Of the eight bathrooms illustrated, all but one depicted the fixtures encased in wooden cabinets. Most hoppers were so well disguised, it was easier to find the fixture by locating its water closet, up near the ceiling. At a time that American kitchens had separate, undisguised elements (eight kitchen sinks in the same catalogue were shown on legs or hung on brackets), the ideal bathroom had matching cabinets enclosing each fixture.

The messages of the cabinets—or lack of them—was clear. One, the closeted convenience was designed for people shy about their bodily functions. Two, the homeowner was too refined to deal with appliances, so the bathroom had not appliances but cabinetry. Servants handled appliances, and the kitchen equipment stood without cabinets because it was for the staff. In the mid-twentieth century, kitchen equipment was encased because the room had become the realm of "the lady of the house," therefore its appliances had to be decorously contained.

One illustration in the 1888 catalogue, "the very complete Bath Room," included a bidet. The rest featured a bathtub (one, a bath-shower combination), a toilet bowl with water closet, a washstand (sink), and a small tub called a "seat bath"—a shallow, 25- by 22-inch tub not unlike many portable tubs then in common use (fig 6.13, the tub at the left). The small tub did not win favor, although it was described as "most useful . . . serving a double purpose, as it is equally well adapted for use as a Foot Bath." A slop sink was suggested only for a children's bathroom, equipped with a child-size tub. Most customers selected three fixtures—the tub, toilet, and sink—and left them freestanding. Yet most Americans in 1888, and into the twentieth century, still used the outdoor privy.

In 1920 the components of the bathroom were essentially the same, and the shower had become an essential. The water closet was lowered to behind the hopper, and footed tubs gave way to built-ins. The built-in tubs gradually shrank, becoming shallower and shorter, and the slope of their backrests diminished. The closeted convenience was still small. The appliances no longer needed names like Purita and Hygeia or Inodoro. Cleanliness, hygiene, and being indoors were now taken for granted.

Fifty years later, the fixtures were still the same. The home improvements most people

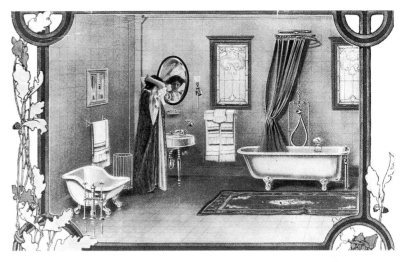

wanted, when they were asked in 1958, was a lavatory or, as it was then known, "a half-bath."[30] Later they wanted the main bathroom larger and a larger tub as well. The resulting room began to read like a site of luxury and indulgence. The sink was back in a cabinet; the room might contain plants, a telephone, perhaps a sitting area and television. Dry heat saunas were briefly in fashion, but it was the bathtubs with water jets, dubbed "spas" or "hot tubs," that became most popular.

Some hot tubs became what baths had been to the Romans, social places, but social places at home. Jacuzzis—developed in the 1960s and first marketed as promoting health—either became bathroom fixtures or recreational tubs in solaria (sunrooms with a name evoking ancient Rome). The 1987 solarium (see fig. 5.11) had a hot tub that was not visible from the kitchen. Japanese bathing was another definite influence, hence wooden tubs, and some tubs went outdoors to decks and patios. Outdoors was where Americans were moving. Within a century of being joyously

Figure 6.13. Advertisement, Standard Manufacturing Co., *House Beautiful,* January 1907. (Cincinnati Historical Society.) The bathroom fixtures, minus the hopper, are depicted in a large sumptuous room with a carpet. By 1907, a shower in the tub was on its way to becoming routine.

welcomed "Inodoro." American plumbing was moving, so to speak, "Outodoro."

THE KITCHEN

Early in the nineteenth century, Benjamin Latrobe thought that the outbuildings in America clustered close by "the dwelling house as a litter of pigs their mother."[31] The structures included privies, barns, icehouses, kitchens, dairies, storehouses, and often more. Of these, the American privy and garage were the last to become part of the main house. The first to move inside was the kitchen.

The earliest manifestations of the kitchen as a room of the English house came shortly before the time of the European settlement. So the American kitchen evolved separately from those in Britain and the Continent. It has been a place for servants, for housewives, and for working couples. It has stood quite segregated from the rest of the house (when it was the servants' realm), has been incorporated into the heart of the living space (as in the hall where Danckaerts prayed in 1680), and has been a semipublic space (the site of a 1950s coffee klatsch).

When someone cooked over a hearth in the center of a castle's hall, the hall was not a kitchen but a multipurpose room in which some cooking was done. Most of the food preparation was done outside. In early-seventeenth-century England—the England that the Pilgrims and Puritans left—the chimney stack was still new. The early settlers had no separate service areas in the house. The first was in the late seventeenth century in the northern colonies, the space in the lean-to along the rear of the house (see fig. 6.2). The kitchen—the cooking room—led the way and revolutionized the home. Multipurpose rooms would become unipurpose.

The lean-to floor plan—often with a three-hearth central chimney—was common in the early eighteenth century. The lean-to was built as part of the original structure or, when its obvious advantage became known, added to existing houses.[32] Several service areas occupied the full width of that lean-to, a large kitchen for food preparation and perhaps small, flanking, unheated rooms: usually a dairy or a buttery, the popular storeroom for bottled ale and other, often bottled, provisions. The buttery was not what the common **fawbit** says, "so named because it held butter and cheese." "Butt" meant "cask," as in wine cask, hence

Figure 6.14. *After the Ride,* undated. (Library of Congress.) The "golden oak" icebox needs the bowl below for collecting the water from the melted ice that runs down the pipe through the box.

"*but*ler." "Buttery" is hardly mentioned after the 1680s (not to say they gave up drink); "dairy" was popular longer; "pantry" was also used. However designated, an unheated room with many shelves on the side of the lean-to kitchen was common.

Cheese, made at home by or under the supervision of the mistress of the house, was stored either in an unheated room in the north-facing lean-to or in the cellar. Sometimes a second, small, unheated room in the lean-to was used as a chamber for a servant. A popular **fawbit:** This was a "borning room," set aside for the woman and her midwife. Inventories do not mention "borning" or "birthing" rooms.

Cold storage was in a cool, damp, dark "root" cellar. The attic was used for drying, and grain was likely to be stored in upstairs chambers, as were Robert Seaver's "Rye, Rye-meale, barley Malt, and Oatmeale" in 1683. The kitchen was not the coordinated space for food preparation that it became in the twentieth century. It relied on many adjunct areas, often not even adjacent. These discrete, disparate spaces were really farm storage places: the elevated, dry, hopefully rodent-resistant attic; the cool dairy; the cool basement, the so-called root cellar for storing produce. These began as separate places on the farm and remained separated spaces in the home for years. To move them all into the cooking room required pantry shelves, kitchen cabinets, and iceboxes (fig. 6.14).

Early in the nineteenth century, ice harvested in New England was shipped to the South; later it came down the Mississippi from ice ponds in Illinois and Wisconsin. In the 1860s, the ice trade accelerated. By the 1920s, the ice might go into one of four compartments in a side-by-side icebox. Although a mechanical electric refrigerator was devised in 1916, gas and then electric refrigerators did not replace the icebox until the 1920s and 1930s and even later. Into the 1930s my grandmother, the one with the five children and the six-drawer bureau, augmented her icebox with a tin coldbox that, in winter, hung on the sill of the kitchen window, looking like a prototype for a window air conditioner but installed at the wrong season.

The American kitchen included an array of devices and appliances. An 1872 cookbook, *Common Sense in the Household* by Marian Harland, decried "the vulgar prejudice against labor-saving machines." Americans agreed and bought equipment aimed at making cooking better and easier: corers and peelers, and eventually food processors and microwave ovens. Easy kitchen domesticity has been an American specialty because, more than in Europe, the kitchen was apt to be where the housewife herself worked. Either she did much of the work or she supervised the kitchen help's activities.

The kitchen remained in the back of the house, where a kitchen door could open to the yard, providing access to the well and to the yard where the refuse was tossed. An additional "summer kitchen" might be out back, at the farthest reach of the house or even outside. Its modern counterparts are the backyard grill and the apartment-terrace hibachi.

What made a room a kitchen was the cooking hearth or stove; a kitchen sink was not a necessity. Water could be toted into the kitchen from a well often just behind the house. In the eighteenth and nineteenth centuries, a copper bowl might be set into the fireplace chimney to hold water to be kept warm by the fire, making warm water for washing readily available. This "warm water bowl" had neither drain nor tap but had to be filled with water from the well. It was not the most convenient system, but the water was warm. In the nineteenth century, water might come up into a standpipe in the cellar, where there would be a sink. Or, later on, it would be hand-pumped up into a kitchen sink.

As soon as the water came into the house, Americans wanted to put a sink in the kitchen. But not the British. English kitchens continued to exclude sinks, and a room was set aside for washing, the scullery. Everything brought into the kitchen was already clean. A German scholar, Hermann Muthesius, noted that even in the late-nineteenth-century English house, "no one would dream of combining the scullery with the kitchen."[33] He said that even in the smallest English cottage, where kitchen and living room were one, there was no kitchen sink. In the United States, it was the sine qua non, as in "everything but . . ."

In the North during the Federal era, the kitchen was sometimes in an ell protruding from the back of the four-room rectangular plan. On a tobacco plantation in December 1852, Olmsted "dined in a room that extended out, rearwardly, from the house" and described

its location as what, in the North, "would have been the kitchen." Instead, the plantation kitchen was a detached log cabin, and the servants brought the dishes "some distance, through the open air [while] the outer door was left constantly open."[34] Other plantation kitchens might match the brick or clapboard of the main house and be attached to it but were at some remove, often below the grade of the main house (fig. 6.15).

A common rationale for the kitchen as a separate structure or for its placement in the rear was the danger of fire. Although fires were frequent, this was more an after-the-fact fawbit than a reason at the time of construction. While fire in an outstructure did not endanger the mansion and one in an ell was less of a threat to the house as a whole, the real reason was comfort. In 1705 a Virginian, Robert Beverley, noted that "all . . . Drudgeries of Cooking, washing, Dairies, &c. are perform'd in Offices detacht from their Dwelling-Houses, which by this means are kept more cool and Sweet."[35] In most areas the ease of expanding to the rear kept kitchens at the back.

Urban kitchens, however, were commonly in the basement, although there a fire would threaten the entire house. When builders' books noted a deficiency to the plan, it was not a concern about fire. Rather, cellar kitchens made for more work and required another servant. Sometimes the dining room was down on the kitchen level, at the front of the house; other cellar kitchens shared the basement with the laundry and drying room or perhaps a servants' hall.

Homeowners repeatedly rebuilt their kitchens. In a small town or a place with a spacious lot, they tacked on yet another kitchen. The most remote room was usually the last in a series of updated kitchens, each probably occasioned by an improvement as Americans went from cooking over wood at the fireplace to using a series of different stoves.

Baking in seventeenth- and eighteenth-centuries kitchens might be a once-a-week job, but it was year-round, in heat or cold. The Federal era saw a start of cooking improvements: a tin oven placed before the fire, then the Rumford stove—a brick enclosure for fireboxes, each independently regulated. Intro-duced in Boston in 1805, it was more widely available after 1811, when Asher Benjamin's *American Builder's Companion* showed Americans how to install Rumford roasters and stoves. By 1820, many a cookstove stood in front of the hearth, but the fireplace was retained for baking.

During the 1830s, freestanding stoves were widely promoted. Yet, Jane Nylander says in *Our Own Snug Fireside*, "despite . . . more than 550 patents issued for cookstoves between the years 1820 and 1850, most authors of cookbooks . . . assumed that cooking would continue to be done on a fireplace with an iron crane, and baking done in a brick oven or on

Figure 6.15. The kitchen at Kenmore, Fredericksburg, Virginia, undated and probably posed. (Library of Congress.) The kitchen floor is brick. The oven is at the left, a "warm water bowl" above it. The crane suspends a kettle over the fire.

the hearth." [36] Many fireplace ovens remained in use through the nineteenth century.

After the Civil War, people bought free-standing rectangular stoves (fig. 6.16) that burned hard coal, soft coal, or wood. Such a stove was sometimes replaced with a freestanding kerosene stove. Later, women cooked with gas or electric on a freestanding range with an oven. By the 1990s, cooking had moved to the built-in range, oven, and microwave, perhaps even a pizza oven, most of it enclosed by cabinets. The English had taken another tack and recessed the stove in the wall, emulating the fireplace. A French chef, however, expected access at the stoveside.

English, continental European, and American kitchens were very different places. European kitchens were solely for food preparation and regarded as totally inappropriate for eating, except possibly by the staff. The narrow galley in most European apartments precluded anything but food storage and preparation. Twentieth-century Americans, however, often chose the work-in, eat-in, sit-in tradition of our early farm kitchens.

As this century began, the kitchen was not even a place to store dishes. China and tableware had long been kept on display in other rooms: on cupboard shelves in the several colonial parlors, then in the Federal dining room. Later, with the proliferation of tableware, sideboard display had to be augmented, and in 1900 a butler's pantry was essential to the operation of both the kitchen and dining room and stood between them. Storage would only become a kitchen function when eating entered the kitchen.

In 1900 the lady of the house might only rarely enter the kitchen. Kitchens were for servants, and while the mistress might review the menu, she had little else to do with all its activities. The Gamble household in Pasadena included five maids, two of whom slept in, a gardener, and a chauffeur, who slept in the garage, a nearby structure with its own fuel pump. James, one of the boys who had slept on the sleeping porch in the 1910s, entered the kitchen for the first time in 1966, when he toured his family home after it was donated to the City of Pasadena. A woman touring a house museum made a similar observation, or the converse, seeing the parlors for the first time, rooms to which she had no access as a servant in the house.

The kitchen that James had never seen was well appointed with meticulously crafted cupboards of light-colored wood: maple and pine. The rest of the woodwork and furniture in the house was dark: mahogany, walnut, stained cedar. Dark wood read as rich. Light woods seemed far less important and, according to a kitchen rationale, were more easily cleaned.

Cleanliness has been a powerful idea in American kitchens. Whitewashed walls, which showed dirt and were easily repainted, seemed sanitary. Yellow was a common color for eighteenth- and nineteenth-century kitchen floors because it showed dirt and was cheap: the pigment came from local clay. White paint, how-ever, came from corroding lead. It was expensive, time-consuming, dangerous to produce, and not made in America until 1801. White-wash was merely lime and water but did not last.

Some floors in the North and South, primarily in kitchens but also in some other rooms, were routinely scoured with and then strewn with light sparkling beach sand. The practice kept floors clean and also pretty. Sylvia King was a slave in Texas when she made corn shuck brooms and decorated floors with them. Years later she was recorded as saying that her mistress liked "floors sanded . . . where you sprinkles fine, white sand over [the] floor and sweeps it round in all kinds purty figgers."[37]

In the name of cleanliness, fashion from time to time called for kitchens to be white or almost entirely white. The black cast-iron kitchen range of the 1890s became the less or-namented white enamel rectangular range on feet of the 1910s, after a brief fling with shiny steel plate ranges. The white stove stood with other freestanding appliances: an icebox, often white; a white kitchen sink on legs, usually with a side drainboard; and a white cupboard. White was considered the "desirable" color for the walls and the painted cupboard. Early-twentieth-century kitchens were to look bright, clean, healthy, and pure. And scientific; home economics was touted as "domestic science."

All was regulated in the kitchen. The Age of Science arrived about 1940 (fig. 6.17). The ideal kitchen counter height was established at 36 inches, a yardstick apparently the standard rather than the cook's height. Efficiency experts mapped out an "ideal arrangement" of the several appliances to conform to ideal working flow patterns. Kitchens were to be designed by engineering experts, not housewives, and tested to see how well they operated. Cabinets with doors were decreed best, closed storage that would protect food, dishes, pots and pans, tableware, and kitchenware from an unhealthy exposure to dirt. The villain was most easily seen and annihilated on white surfaces. Dirt equaled germs.

A century had passed since Catharine Beecher wrote *A Treatise on Domestic Economy* (1841). When she and her sister, Harriet Beecher Stowe, wrote *The American Woman's Home* in 1869, they sought to revolutionize the kitchen and the home. Reformers and feminists suggested that the private kitchen was as dated as the spinning wheel and should be abolished. Less than 5 percent of women worked outside the home in 1890, but reformers sought to take advantage of technology, then producing elevators, improved gas stoves, gas refrigerators, vacuum cleaners, and washing machines. All, however, were large, for commercial use only. Reformers devised apartment houses that functioned as communities with central housekeeping facilities. European apartment houses adopted common laundries and drying rooms based on such thinking.

Americans, however, demurred. They preferred their private realm and kept the family kitchen. Americans made the labor-saving tools smaller and individually affordable. The family washing machine, ironically, did not save labor. It kept dirty linen at home, which doomed commercial laundries that thrived in the first half of the twentieth century by serving housewives without laundresses. Apartment dwellers generally eschewed common drying rooms, hanging laundry out the window or in the bathtub.

From the start, the bathroom served as an adjunct to the kitchen. Before the refrigerator, fish stayed fresh by staying alive. My grandmother's bathtub held swimming carp that was about to become gefilte fish, a small indoor reflection of Jefferson's oval fish pond just beyond the kitchen dependency at Monticello. Even in homes with a refrigerator, the bathroom might serve as a kitchen adjunct. My mother's neighbor, an immigrant from Greece, drained yogurt over her bathtub, suspending it as she would damp laundry, using her bathroom as a colonist did her lean-to or cellar dairy.

Some Americans traded kitchen white for color, gaiety, and woodiness in the mid-1920s, hearkening back to the prescientific kitchen. Color and wood said "homey" and made for a "farm kitchen" or "country kitchen," a room enshrined in American memories and extolled in family reminiscences. Mid-nineteenth-century farm kitchens had been large rooms, often used for sitting as well as food preparation. There, family and farmhands ate or gathered around the wood or coal stove of an evening. It might be the site of group chores: corn husking, apple paring, productive socials whose names changed with the activity: "apple frolic," "sewing bee." A romantic view of the past was created with shelves of pewter, unpainted wood surfaces, and perhaps a spinning wheel.

In kitchens without servants, cabinetry covered appliances, and the family came to a kitchen table to eat. People without breakfast rooms wanted breakfast nooks in the kitchens; apartment house kitchens got dinettes. Since then, real estate ads have touted the desirable American kitchen as "eat-in."

After 1950, wood cabinets created a built-in, unified appearance. If the surface was plastic laminate instead of wood, the laminate looked like wood and was named accordingly (e.g., Formica's Luxwood). Cabinet woods were often dark, such as those used in the Gamble house everywhere but in the kitchen. The wood made it clear that the people in the kitchen were housewives, not servants. By 1970, a desk might be incorporated in the cabinetry, a place for housewifery: writing recipes and shopping lists and paying bills. Such desks ceased to be featured within two decades. The wife chose to write elsewhere; she was not staying put in "her" room.

In the late twentieth century, while Europe extolled the scientific kitchen (in America, "a continental kitchen" meant shiny metal and white plastic), most Americans continued their by-then-fanciful notion that they lived in a nation of farmers. The homey wooden cabinets in the kitchen-eating-social room enclosed a growing number of appliances.

The clothes washer and dryer often joined the dishwasher in the kitchen or just off it, in the mud room. As the nineteenth-century English suspected—and Muthesius reported—only the worst would follow when a sink entered the kitchen. So, without sculleries, uncouth Yan-

kees brought their dirty clothing into the cooking room.

Appliances proliferated and hummed. Even with the food-preparing mechanisms, much of the food entered the kitchen already prepared. Some hot food could be prepared at the sink: a new tap dispensed boiling hot water, previously available only from a kettle suspended from the fireplace crane or sitting on the stove. The clear separation of roles that the English had seen between stove and sink was obliterated. Dehydrated instant food—from soup to tea (if not nuts)—became food by drawing water. This tap gave new meaning to "the kitchen sink." The term had told *where* the sink was, not *what* it was. But "kitchen" meant cooking before it meant the cooking room. With boiling water on tap, the "kitchen sink" became a "cooking sink."

In the 1990s, the once-shunned sink mul-

Figure 6.17. Mrs. Rogan and her son in the kitchen, Franklin Terrace, Erie, Pennsylvania, new wartime housing built near the General Electric Co. plant where Mr. Rogan was a drill-press operator, 1941. (Library of Congress.) Mrs. Rogan has standard appliances: a four-burner stove with an oven, a refrigerator, counter workspace with cabinets below, and a double sink for washing dishes on the left and laundry on the right. The lack of doors on the cupboard is the only sign of economizing.

tiplied. The turn-of-the-century English cook, who wouldn't deign to do her skullery maid's work, would be aghast. The mistress and the master of the American house worked at the kitchen sink—or sinks. Even after dishwashers removed that chore from monopolizing kitchen sinks, one did not always suffice, so a second was installed in or near the kitchen, a sort of butler's sink, often called a "bar" sink. Two sinks plus dishwasher became America's kitchen ideal.

Which brings us to where we were at the end of Chapter 2, sitting on barstools at the kitchen counter. In front of us, across the counter—the kitchen. Behind us—the impressive view from the kitchen. Closest to the kitchen, the dining room—no longer a room necessarily, but a dining "area," a section of a larger living space. The open space beyond—some real estate brokers dubbed it "the great room"—was the sitting room, family room, living room. Its glass doors led out to a porch, terrace, patio, or garden, or to a vista of garden, golf course, pool, landscape, or skyline. The kitchen with the great view was clearly not designed for a servant. Nor for a housewife alone. This room was for the family.

All that divided the kitchen from the house's best view was a counter or a pseudo-table half-wall that arrived in the 1950s as a hole in the wall called a "pass-through." A small hole at first, it enabled food to be passed easily from the kitchen to the dining room, thus serving the nonservant household much as the dumbwaiter had lifted meals from the cellar kitchen to the first-floor dining room. The small opening breached the wall that since the late seventeenth century had shut off the service kitchen. The woman of the house—in the 1950s it still was the woman—got to peek out. But she wanted more.

At the same time, the dining room was being absorbed into the living room, into an elongated room or an L-shaped space. The housewife at the pass-through was tempted by the sights and sounds of family and guests. When glass walls opened the house at the rear, when Americans and their porches moved around to the back of the house, seeing into the dining-living area often meant seeing through to the outdoors. The partitioning wall between kitchen and dining room came down in favor of a counter and a kitchen with a view, and the kitchen rejoined the dining-living space (see fig. 5.11).

So emerged the late-twentieth-century's cooking-eating-dining-sitting room. Or, rather, cooking-eating-dining-sitting-sleeping room. Shades of the seventeenth-century hall. There was no bed in the piano, but perhaps there was one in the couch. The room had a hearth, sometimes a fireplace or stove, but certainly the family hearth known as the TV. The meal being heated behind the counter might be a contemporary of the pass-through: in 1953, America got its first TV dinner. ❇

CHAPTER 7

THIS IS THE PLACE
REGIONAL DESIGN

A merica is a place of many places. Regionalism in design is not unique to this country, but here it has been unrivaled. We will visit places from the Northeast to Southern California, pausing on the mid-Atlantic coast, in the South, Midwest, and Southwest. We start, however, in Devonshire. England, in a town called Ottery-St.-Mary.

THE CRAFTSMAN'S LEGACY

Grace Cole (1636–1686) married William Searle (1634–1667), a joiner, in Ottery-St.-Mary in 1659.[1] The newlyweds soon left for New England, going first to Boston. By marrying and then emigrating, they followed a pattern: craftsmen tended to delay marriage until they had a trade and to embark for a new life in America shortly thereafter. By 1663, the Searles were in Ipswich, a coastal town north of Boston and south of Portsmouth, where William signed a note as part of a financial transaction with another joiner, Thomas Dennis (1638–1706) of Portsmouth.

Working with a few scant documents and distinctive carvings, furniture scholars have cobbled together the relationships between the Searles and Dennis, between Ipswich and Ottery-St.-Mary, Devonshire. Devonshire craftsmen produced some of the finest carved woodwork and plasterwork then in England. The similar motifs on Ipswich furniture (fig.7.1) were among the finest in New England. Comparing the two showed that Searle was well versed in Devonshire designs and, in Ipswich, continued to carve as he had in England.

Figure 7.1. Carving detail on oak box, William Searle or Thomas Dennis, Ipswich, Massachusetts, 1663–1680. The full-height detail shows the central motif, one third of the box façade. Had it been carved in Ottery-St.-Mary, England, it would look the same.

Grace Cole Searle played a central role in this story about design and place. After her husband died, she married Dennis, who moved from Portsmouth to Ipswich. He, too, may have trained in Devonshire, and may have known Searle there. They evidently shared designs and techniques, and at least Dennis trained apprentices and sons, making the attribution of furniture to one or the other of Grace Cole's husbands difficult.

What is important to us is the family connection. Often a trade or position such as town minister passed from father to son, from father to apprentice and son-in-law, or through marriage, from deceased husband to next husband. Familial ties enhanced the influence of a craftsman in his locale. Searle's wares apparently found a market in Ipswich, for Dennis moved there; the widow didn't move to Portsmouth. Once married, in October 1668, Dennis continued Searle's design tradition in the same locale, and so extended these designs beyond the life of one man. Family ties could leave a craftsman's mark on his town for generations.

All fashion, like politics, was local—seventeenth-century fashion in widely separated communities especially so. Settlers usually brought along a blacksmith and a woodworker. William Russell (1612–1648/49) and William Gibbons (d. 1689) were recruited in London in 1640 to join the New Haven Colony. New Haven's fashionable inlaid joinery was readily discernible from Boston's version of high-style London of the same time.

The Plymouth Colony enjoyed an architectural style rich in moldings and applied turnings (see fig. 1.14). So did Boston, but its looked different from Plymouth joinery, lacking the distinctive sawtooth moldings. By 1635 Bostonians could get high-style London joinery from Ralph Mason (1599–1678/79), a new arrival from London, and sophisticated turnings from Thomas Edsall (1588–1676), whose family were turners in London.

Fashionable Boston and Plymouth furniture had an architectural style, with moldings and applied turnings. These designs eschewed the older, carved decoration. Inland, at Wethersfield and elsewhere along the Connecticut River, the joinery combined architectural moldings, turnings, and carvings as well (see fig. 2.9).

In smaller towns, carved decoration was in fashion. Searle, who apparently found no market in Boston for his carved style, succeeded in Ipswich. South of Boston, along the North River, settlers bought furniture from joiners whose carving traditions came from elsewhere in Britain, especially Norfolk. Within a short distance of a principal town were communities with their own styles, each distinguishable from the urban style and each recognizable as from its own community. The carving style in the Hingham-Scituate area, south of Boston (see the toilet table and box, figs. 1.5 and 1.9), was decidedly different from that in Ipswich. So, within a few years of the Great Migration of the 1630s, the English in a small part of America had distinct regional designs.

Individual craftsmen, especially early immigrants, left legacies of style as well as objects. They brought to a place a look that came to define it at least as much as its location on the map and its climate. And Americans came from all over. The settling community would be important in a "New Sweden." Swede Point was not going to look like St. Augustine, nor New Amsterdam like New Haven. No matter how few their number, no matter when they settled here, immigrants across the country made their mark, and their influence endured.

Townsfolk, patronizing their local craftsman and familiar with his work, usually preferred it to anything else except perhaps a London import. Craftsmen coming into a town had to compete with or adopt the established local style. Motifs, such as the sawtooth design, pervaded all the community's furniture, the fashionable and the ordinary. The joiner supplied a broad variety of goods: expensive work for those willing and able to pay for it, barely ornamented wares in the same style for customers with humble tastes or purses. Thus, well before 1700, each New England settlement had a look that said, "This is the place." For Englishmen so far from home, that must have felt good.

CRAFTSMAN, PATRON, AND THE COMPETITION

Throughout the eighteenth century, European America remained a place of places where each community drove its own style. Only a few people knew what was in fashion elsewhere in America, let alone in England. Most craftsmen were born here and locally trained, but those who had trained abroad were influential. In urban centers, craftsmen trained in America were eager to learn from the new immigrants. A century after Dennis left Portsmouth for Ipswich and Grace Searle, another immigrant arrived in the New Hampshire capital and revolutionized its style. His story exemplifies the impact of one craftsman on others in the town.

Occasionally a town was ready for a new look to go with its new prosperity or its new image of itself. Portsmouth was such a place in 1765. Even its craftsmen were ready for something new, something better, when a skilled cabinetmaker arrived whose work perfectly suited the atmosphere in the prosperous port.

Robert Harrold (d. 1792) arrived in 1765, when the colony had recently expanded inland and was enjoying a dramatic increase in its timber trade. The houses in Portsmouth were extraordinarily commodious, often three stories high, and of fine quality. During the early 1760s, building expanded; Portsmouth timber merchants even exported entire house frames to the Caribbean. Town carpenters turned to design books for ideas for the elegant interior woodwork that ornamented the splendid new dwellings.

Portsmouth furniture, however, was another matter. Not until 1763 did the town have its first professional upholsterer. Before then, seat frames had to be shipped to Boston. So Boston furniture was imported, some English

cosmopolitans demanding European embellishments. The local clientele, patronizing local craftsmen, was the base from which the craftsmen in the thriving city built their trade. But they also reached out to a wealthy elite all over America, especially in the South, in the booming port of New Orleans, for example, and in southern and Caribbean plantations. This clientele patronized a few select firms such as Belter and Herter. They entertained in French rococo or Renaissance drawing rooms and sought titled Europeans as mates for their daughters. A sort of late-nineteenth-century version of the twentieth-century's jet set, they looked well beyond the borders of any one locale, and their taste went beyond regionalism.

So the New Orleans hotelier Ruggles Morse (1816–1893) built his summer home in Portland, Maine, to plans by a Connecticut architect and ordered furniture and other decorations from New York's Gustave Herter (see fig. 3.10, the drawing room). Morse and his wife were born in Maine; he began his career in Boston, honed his skills in New York, and made a fortune in New Orleans, a boom town to which he moved in the mid-1840s. Nothing was regional about the Morses' taste or the interiors that Herter designed for them.

Such elegance as was seen in the Morses' parlor appealed to the wealthy socialites in the new metropolises—in San Francisco for one, in Chicago for another. Belter parlor suites, Herter bedroom sets, and other expensive and elaborate furniture left New York warehouses for new cities and towns perhaps named Athens, Paris, or Rome, so great were their cit-izens' aspirations. (The United States has eleven Athenses, nine Parises, and six Romes.) Harriet Martineau chided Americans for their nomenclature: "We not only find [in New York] Utica, Syracuse, Manlius, and Camillus, [but] Geneva on Seneca Lake, with Ithaca at its other extremity." [14] In towns so named, Main Street could have a Grand Hotel and an Opera House, and the elite could furnish their homes with New York's best. Would regionalism vanish from America?

The Erie Canal replaced the Iroquois Trail in 1825. Barge canals more than facilitated travel inland for people crossing New York State and did wonders for moving products. Canals provided craftsmen with another route for their furniture and furniture styles. Rails augmented then rerouted water-based trade routes, and late-nineteenth-century New York furniture was shipped to San Francisco while modest Grand Rapids furniture sold in Dallas. A coast-to-coast north-south unity of design seemed possible but did not appear. Instead, a new design region developed along the railroad line, where towns clung to the identity acquired the day the first train came through.

HEADING WEST: CROSSROADS AND RIVER JUNCTIONS

The regionalism that left its stamp on the original thirteen states migrated westward into Ohio, a place of diverse places, a sort of national crossroads of rivers and canals. Different peoples left distinct marks in Ohio, and local pride kept each heritage alive. Northeasterners brought a rather faithful version of New England to the Western Reserve; northeastern Ohio was called "New Connecticut" in the early nineteenth century. Virginians recreated another Virginia in Ohio just south of the Western Reserve and just beyond what became West Virginia. In the twentieth century their communities reflected those Yankee and Virginia origins. Meanwhile, Germans from Pennsylvania brought their own tradition to Ohio, including the doored cabinet. Lawrence Allwine, a Windsor chairmaker from Philadelphia, settled in Zanesville, Ohio, about 1800 and there continued to produce Windsors, apparently even continuing to mark his products "L. Allwine Philadᵃ" (much as Lannuier kept his Paris connection).

French settlers came from Canada, via Lake Erie, and put French curves on their Ohio furniture. Along the northern Mississippi, the Ohio, and the Wabash were towns named Versailles (western Ohio), Terre Haute and Vincennes (western Indiana), as well as St. Louis. After the French troops withdrew and Anglo populations arrived, the communities kept their French character and their connections among themselves and with French Canada. A buffet (fig. 7.10), a form most Americans would have called a sideboard, looks as if it came from the Manche district of Normandy. Used in Terre Haute, it apparently was made in Vincennes, where most people had French-Canadian ties. There, someone wanting French carvings and curves was apt to find a cabinetmaker working in the French tradition. The hazards and costs of shipping furniture helped strengthen local designs, but customer taste and craftsman

know-how ruled. If one paid the freight, it was always possible to order what one truly wanted from the man who could really make it.

A small community settling in a small area

Figure 7.10. Buffet, poplar and maple, H: 46¼"; W: 48"; D: 24¼". Wabash River Valley, Indiana, perhaps by Pierre Antoine Petit, called La Lumiere, Vincennes, ca. 1800. (Museum of Fine Arts, Boston.) Until the 1920s, the buffet was in Terre Haute. Its abstract egg-and-dart design around the drawers, the shape of the foot, and the joinery (note the paneled case side) is typical of Manche, Normandy.

imprinted a style and a few new residents were inclined to adopt it, but a large number of immigrants settling in a large river valley made their style widespread. When the Mississippi was a French river, its environs were sparsely settled. Then the valley—the farmlands of the entire Midwest—became the home of large numbers of northern Europeans, mostly Germans, and Easterners looking for space and opportunity. The many German immigrants in the early and mid-nineteenth century brought to the Midwest a middle-class German style called "Biedermeier," an everyman's version of neoclassical design.

Biedermeier was a pale adaptation of the

gilded Napoleonic grandeur made by Lannuier. It included light wood examples, such as the sophisticated Cincinnati secretary (fig. 7.11), which invites comparison with the Quervelle (see fig. 7.8), dark wood examples like the walnut bed made in Texas (fig. 7.12), and rude furniture in frontier cabins. The style, usually rendered in light or modest woods, featured robust cornices and scrolls, was trim and neat, and had clean lines and gentle curves (as in fig. 7.15, a Texas settee). A style that aimed to avoid the extravagant was ideal for the frontier. Germans also brought to Texas and the Mississippi River valley the practice of using doored cabinets, including a wardrobe, the *Schrank*,

akin to the *kas*. Before wardrobes became popular elsewhere in late-nineteenth-century America, they were staples in the houses of German-Americans or in areas settled by Germans.

As northeastern Ohio looked east and southeastern Ohio looked southeast, Cincinnati, in the southwest corner, looked down the Ohio and Mississippi rivers to the many German newcomers in the river valley. A trading center from its founding at the turn of the nineteenth century, Cincinnati was across the Ohio River from Kentucky and, as the water flows, very near Indiana, Illinois, Missouri, Arkansas, Tennessee, and Mississippi. A bit farther downriver was Louisiana, with its world port of New Orleans. (Cincinnati lost some of its German flavor when America entered World War I. Streets named "German," "Bremen," and "Berlin" suddenly became "English," "Republic," and "Woodrow.")

From Cincinnati south to Texas and west beyond Milwaukee into the Dakotas, the Biedermeier style thrived among the immigrant farm population. Settlers bought the modest German version of neoclassical and produced it. Johann Umland (b. 1811) arrived in Texas in 1849, a year after his older brother, Heinrich.[15] Both were cabinetmakers in Hamburg. Heinrich owned a shop employing from six to twelve workers, but the business was ruined by the fire of 1848 and the subsequent economic depression as political upheaval spread across Germany. Arriving in America, Heinrich became a farmer and when he died in 1868 owned 175 acres, horses, cattle, and oxen. But Johann, who made the four-poster (fig. 7.12), continued making furniture in Washington County, Texas, until 1880.

Europe's unrest, such as that in 1848, and ill fortune prompted many family migrations and many new farming careers. It also brought to America hands skilled in the furniture trades. Gustave Herter, the German cabinet-maker who settled in New York City and set a new standard for fashionable interiors, was among the "forty-eighters."

Scandinavians, such as the Swedes who settled in Iowa and Minnesota, felt at home with the simplified neoclassical style that they, too, had known in northern Europe. Attracted by farmlands, the Scandinavians brought their trunks, their rosemaling tradition, their folk designs, and their preference for neoclassical curves without the gilt. Biedermeier simplicity suited their modest farmhouses. So many immigrants came to America for farmland that mid-nineteenth-century America developed a farm country style, and its idealized image has persisted.

Cincinnati's assets—its water paths, forests, and, in the midcentury, steam power—made it a furniture capital whose principal market was the growing Mississippi Valley. Via rivers and canals, factories disseminated neoclassical furniture and "fancy chairs," as decoratively painted Windsors were known, throughout the Midwest. The industry enjoyed the advantage of surrounding cherry, walnut, maple, sycamore, and poplar forests. Furniture firms brought pine in from Pittsburgh and mahogany from New Orleans. In the 1840s, when the factories turned to steam power to mini-

mize handwork, they cut prices by a third. Cincinnati had 48 cabinetmaking factories and 11 chair factories in 1841 and, a decade later, 136 factories, employing 1,158 workers. There Charles Hess, probably of German extraction, put a bed in a piano in 1866.

A JOURNEY SOUTH

In the American South every locale, whether in town or on a plantation, was a place divided with precision between rich and poor, between mansions (such as the Charleston homes of the several Manigaults) and workers' dwellings, which ranged from overseers' houses to slave housing. The houses of most

Figure 7.12. Bed, walnut and pine, Johann Umland, Chappell Hill, Texas, 1861. (Winedale Museum, Roundtop, Texas.) Umland made this bed for a rancher, Terrell J. Jackson. Typical of late German Biedermeier style, it is far more sophisticated than most Texas furniture.

freed blacks and poor whites fell somewhere between those of overseer and slave.

Our views of the scene come through the eyes of Frederick Law Olmsted well before he designed New York City's Central Park. From 1852 to 1854 he traveled through the South and drew word-pictures of what he observed, including those log houses without any "glass windows" and the muslin curtains that kept bugs out, depictions so fine that the reader of his *Cotton Kingdom* barely regrets that there was no camera. In Louisiana he arrived at a "first-rate plantation," whose "large and handsome mansion . . . had not been occupied for several years." The overseer had not seen the owner in more than two years. Empty mansions were common, usually for shorter periods, while the family spent the social season in the city. The owners picked up and moved, not unlike the royal Plantagenets on their circuit, carrying their household in trunks hither and thither. That was how Harriet Manigault was caught keyless in Philadelphia.

The overseer of the cotton plantation that Olmsted visited had charge of "135 slaves, big and little . . . 67 went to the field regularly" plus "3 mechanics (blacksmith, carpenter, and wheelwright), 2 seamstresses, 1 cook, 1 stable servant, 1 cattle tender, 1 hog tender, 1 teamster, 1 house servant (overseer's cook) and one midwife and nurse . . . and a driver of the hoe gang . . . and a foreman of the plow gang." The cabin of the white overseer and his wife was larger than those in the "large Negro 'settlement,'" and Olmsted dined there on cold cornbread and fat bacon. The wife apologized for not making coffee; the cook had gone to bed. After a slave stabled Olmsted's horse and brought wood for a fire, she set a chair for their guest in front of it. The fireside, often surrounded by unpainted and unpapered log walls (fig. 7.13), was the true focal point in log houses throughout the lower Mississippi valley.

Olmsted recorded a clear picture of their bedroom:

I think they gave up their one bed to me, for it was a double, and had been slept in since the sheets were last changed; the room was garnished with pistols and other arms and ammunition, rolls of Negro cloth, shoes and hats, handcuffs, a large medicine chest, and several books on medical and surgical subjects and farriery; while articles of both men's and women's wearing apparel hung against the wall, which were also decorated with some large patent medicine posters.

Such posters were popular decoration in the area at that time.

Many southern whites and emancipated slaves lived more poorly. A cabin on Olmsted's route across Mississippi and Alabama

comprised in a single room, twenty-eight by twenty-five feet . . . open to the roof above . . . a large fireplace at one end and a door on each side—no windows at all. Two bedsteads, a spinning-wheel, a packing case, which served as a bureau, a cupboard, made of rough hewn slabs, two or three deerskin seated chairs, a Connecticut clock, and a

Figure 7.13. Interior of a log cabin, eastern Oklahoma, ca. 1900. (University of Oklahoma.) The cabin with its well-equipped hearth is furnished like the overseers' cabins Olmsted saw a half century earlier.

large poster of Jayne's patent medicine, constituted all the visible furniture.

There Olmsted slept on one of the two bedsteads; the family—husband, wife, young daughter, and infant—slept on the floor on bedding taken from the other. All were plagued by gnats, although the woman had prepared a smoking brazier of embers and corncobs to drive them out, placing it on the sill of one of the two open doorways—the windward door. There it "burned feebly and smoked lustily, like an altar to the Lares, all night," while the cabin was so open that the smoke itself gave but "little annoyance."[16]

Slave cabins were smaller and ruder. Roughly made of logs—chinked with whatever came to hand, corn shuck or cotton wad—the poorest had one room, ten or twelve foot square, with a fireplace, one door, and often no window openings. No trees, no porch, no shade of any kind. About five people slept in bunks attached to the wall. When the trundles or pallets for youngsters were in use, there was often no room to step on the floor.

Mattresses or pallets on the floor were stuffed with wheat straw or corn shucks, and an occasional chicken feather pillow might be made by a resourceful kitchen slave. The beds—and the table, if there was one—were usually two-legged affairs affixed to the wall and known to Texans as "Georgia horses." Andy Marion, who as a slave had lived in a cabin with a dirt floor in South Carolina, called them "contraptions": "They bored auger holes in [the] sides of [the] room, stuck end of poles in [the] holes. [Each pole stuck] out into room and rested on wooden blocks sort of hollowed out on top; then some slats of pine finish up [the] contraption."[17]

Among the best slave dwellings was a double cabin, whitewashed, of frame and board and plastered within,

forty-two feet long, twenty-one feet wide, divided into two family tenements, each twenty-one by twenty-one; each tenement divided into three rooms—one . . . twenty-one by ten; each of the others [bedrooms], ten by ten . . . a brick fireplace in the middle of the long [wall of the] living room . . . a cock loft. [reached by ladder from the main room] . . . a front and back door, and each room a window closed by a wooden shutter, swinging outward, on hinges.[18]

Palings surrounded a small plot with a garden, chicken coop, and perhaps a sow. Sparse homemade furniture was common, hand-me-down furniture from the big house prized. Plank floors were usual, but dirt floors were also common. Slave housing in Louisiana was apt to have a long front porch.

In Tennessee, Olmsted found all the poor farmers wearing homespun so that "a spinning-wheel is heard in every house [see the woman at a great wheel, fig. 2.15], and frequently a loom is clanging in the gallery, always worked by women." He was very pleased to find lodging in "a large, neat, white house, with Negro shanties, and an open log cabin in the front yard." Approaching on a June evening, he saw a "stout, elderly, fine-looking woman . . . upon the gallery, fanning herself. Two little Negroes had just brought a pail of fresh water, and she was drinking of it with a gourd." Invited to put his saddlebags safely in "the parlor," he noted: "The interior of the house was furnished with unusual comfort. 'The parlor,' however, had a bed in it." This arrangement—principal bed in principal room—that had been standard in American homes into the eighteenth century caught Olmsted by surprise.

As Olmsted and the woman spoke on the front porch, her husband arrived; he spoke first with his wife about the hot weather and only then "squared his chair towards [Olmsted] threw it back so as to recline against the post, and said gruffly, 'Good evening, sir.'"

The cabin in the front yard was the kitchen, and there the family's two daughters served supper "assisted by the two little Negro boys." At breakfast the next morning, a slave woman would serve and the daughters would sit at the table. When Olmsted retired after dinner, "The master held a candle for me while I undressed, in a large room above stairs; and gave me my choice of the four beds." Later, an older son joined him in the room, not bothering to take off his clothes to sleep.

When Olmsted went downstairs in the morning, "having been wakened early by flies, and the dawn," he "saw the master lying on his bed in the 'parlor,' still asleep in the clothes he wore at supper. His wife was washing her face on the gallery, being already dressed for the day." After she used what Olmsted called "the family towel," she retrieved her smoking pipe and took her place on the porch chair at the doorway. Olmsted was shocked by their way of living. "Yet everything betokened an opulent

Figure 7.14 Front porch of a mountain cabin, photograph by Margaret Morley, western North Carolina, 1910–1913. (North Carolina Archives.) The porch furnishings include a washstand with bowl and ladle.

and prosperous man—rich land, extensive crops, a number of Negroes, and considerable herds of cattle and horses. He also had capital invested in mines and railroads, he told me."[19]

Staying overnight in that populous and poor valley, Olmsted saw the life of a well-to-do family—bed in the parlor, toilet performed on the porch (fig.7.14; note the washstand at the left), supper in the kitchen—as no mere passerby would have observed. (Hotels have deprived historians of such records as might have been written by later Danckaerts and Olmsteds.) Why did Olmsted's Tennessee hosts live as they did? Was it the regional style? Perhaps, in their valley, they knew no other way. West of the Appalachians, they apparently did not traditionally "do the season" in the city as plantation owners east of the mountains—Virginians, Carolinians, and Georgians—did. Isolated, they apparently lacked both the enlarged community and the sense of style that was afforded by periods of city life.

Even field slaves had chances to extend their community beyond the plantation they worked. A slave in Texas recalled taking part each year in some ten or more communal corn shuckings, where slaves from miles around were gathered together. While shucking four or five hundred ears of corn in a single session, they relished the sense of expanded community, made social connections, and gained a wider regional identity.

TEXAS

In eastern Texas in the 1850s, a two-story log cabin with glass windows was a substantial house. Western Texas was the frontier being settled by immigrant Germans and Southerners, and log cabins were the homes of America's frontiers. Caroline Mackensen Romberg

pensive teawares securely. As a consequence of its value, all of it, of course, had to be prominently on display. A tea table at which to serve was a necessity. Often a second tea table permanently held the tea service. In the Saywards' remodeled parlor (see fig. 7.6), the round table near the corner and the rectangular table at the left were both for tea.

At the time of the Revolution, the colonists focused on the thruppence tax on a pound of Chinese tea, which the Crown insisted be shipped through England.

Farewell the teaboard with its gaudy
    equipage
Of cups and saucers, creambucket, sugar
    tongs.
The pretty tea-chest, also lately stored
With Hyson. Congo and best double fine.
Full many a joyous moment have I sat by ye
Hearing the girls tattle, the old maids talk
    scandal.[4]

The farewell to the "teaboard," a tea tray sometimes permanently set on a tea table, was premature. Tea drinking had so completely won the hearts of American women that it seemed a necessity. The rebels who dumped the English shipments of tea into Boston Harbor were not trying to end the practice that had, within a lifetime, become such a universally beloved custom. Instead, they encouraged women to make tea of other crops, including loosestrife, a purple weed that still clogs New England marshes in the summer. In broadsides, newspapers, and songs, they called on young ladies to forsake Bohea and Green Hyson in favor of Labrador and Liberty tea.

So women drank water boiled with leaves that had never before been used for tea. They also took to drinking coffee at home. On July 31, 1777, Abigail Adams wrote of "a great Scarcity of Sugar and Coffe, articles which the Female part of the State are very loth to give up."[5] They had already given up Chinese tea. After the war they resumed drinking tea, as Mrs Humphreys's portrait shows, and drank coffee in their parlors as well.

The men's complaints about teawares make it clear that women were the customers. Teawares expanded the realm of female consumerism beyond the world of "Sugar and Coffe," foodstuffs and linens, into chinaware, silverware, and furniture.

"ORIENTAL" TO OCCIDENTAL EYES

Design changed rapidly during the tea-drinking years, in part a consequence of tea drinking, tea socials, and shifting ideas of what seemed to be Chinese. The English and their colonists wanted so many things to be in, as they said, "the Chinese taste."

A "Tea Pot a la mode" was derided but rather clearly depicted in this 1754 description: "Strange beasts were drawn in taste Chinese. / And frightful Fish and hump-backed Trees."[6] European ceramics also looked Chinese. Blue and white delft was made in Delft to look like the blue and white canton imported from Canton. Europeans put handles on their teacups and changed their shape but still thought they looked Chinese by virtue of their

surface decoration. Porcelain was called "china." English worsteds made to resemble Chinese fabric designs were called "Cheney" or "China."

Tea equipage, precious stuff that it was, was rendered in silver. Covered silver sugar bowls took the form of covered ceramic rice bowls. Silversmiths took their clues for the shape of teapots from globular Chinese porcelain pots, making their teapots as round as if turned on a potter's wheel. Not until the Federal era, when the Chinese hold on design had loosened, did people want teapots shaped like Roman urns, as Mrs. Humphreys's was. Silversmiths engraved their teapots—and soon tankards and toiletry items as well—with Chinese images similar to the "frightful Fish and hump-backed Trees" on Chinese ceramics.

In some homes, the entire parlor assumed an Oriental cast. To Occidental eyes, that is.

Figure 8.2. Tea table set for guests. (Winterthur Museum.) The grouping of furniture in Winterthur's Readbourne Parlor resembles a setting in a mid-eighteenth-century bedchamber. The japanned chest is from Boston, 1740–1750; the tea table, side chairs, and easy chair from Philadelphia.

Snippets of design came from anywhere between Persia and Japan. The colonists showed off their most elegant equipage in the best parlor, but they also wanted teawares and some Chinese fashion in other rooms of the house. Chinese wallpapers were available to wealthy merchants and plantation owners, and a few turned their parlors into splendid Chinese fantasies with papers and textiles. Almost all the colonists acquired new parlor tables on which to display their china or silver teawares to the greatest advantage. Surely in such a setting one could not ask guests to sit on old-fashioned chairs. Ideally the whole room was in or appropriate to "the Chinese taste."

Neither customers nor fabricators had ever seen any Chinese furniture. Nevertheless, many objects were faintly Chinese, more in-the-spirit than authentic. To suggest sufficed. What counted was creating an appropriate aura in which to imbibe a Chinese drink. The colonists achieved the desired effect by placing some exotic Chinese design elements here and there: the body-conforming S-curve of the splat, any splat, and S-curved outlines, and, after mid-century, fretwork and straight, unturned legs. In addition, lacquered furniture (such as the high chest in fig. 8.2), most of it made in Boston, featured what seemed to be Chinese figures and landscapes.

Bits of these European and colonial furniture designs make it clear that someone at some time had seen something that actually was Chinese. For example, the walnut tea table made in York, Maine (fig. 8.3), was apparently the one that the Saywards relegated to the sitting room in the 1760s, when they redid the parlor in mahogany and Boston style. This older tea table bears an uncanny resemblance to a small tea table (fig. 8.4) made in China during the Ming dynasty, probably about the time the Portuguese got Macao. But neither it nor anything like it is known, or even believed, to have been brought to the United States until the nineteenth century.

TEA AND OTHER TABLES, AND TIMBER

Western tea tables originated about the start of the eighteenth century, when tea was new to the colonies. After 1720, with all that precious equipage needing a safe stand, at least

one tray-edged table was a necessity in a stylish household. Unlike with ceramic wares, however, there were no Chinese examples to imitate. A cargo of tea tables on tall legs could not be stacked tightly and shipped efficiently, and space in the hold of a trading ship was at a premium.

Trays, with a lipped or galleried edge to protect the wares being carried, were more likely to have been early imports from China. Upper-class English already used serving trays. However, the manifests of the East India Company do not show trays as significant cargo. Trays were less common in the colonies.

The very first tables used for tea were probably other stands or small tables in general use, tables that since the early settlements had their own American look. In the colonies, small household tables, often called tavern tables but actually used anywhere, usually looked different from their English counterparts. Long before American Windsors went their own way with distinctive splayed legs because of the abundant native woods, American tabletops stretched out to new dimensions—for the same reason. Overhanging tops became a design preference, as splayed Windsor legs would, but they originated because of the wood.

Colonial joiners discovered almost at once that they did not have to piece chest lids together, for the available pine timbers provided for one- or two-board chest lids. Similarly mill-sawn pine boards enabled the joiners to create expansive tabletops that were far larger than their joined bases. John Kirk, in *Ameri-*

Figure 8.5. Tea table, cherry, H: 27"; W: 31⅝"; D: 20½". Wethersfield, Connecticut, 1760–1780. (Webb-Deane-Stevens Museum.) Originally owned by Thomas Belden of Wethersfield. The scalloped top never had a molded edge.

can Furniture & the British Tradition, neatly describes English tabletops as tending to "hug the dimensions of the supporting frame."[7] That cannot be said of American tabletops or of the Massachusetts bench (see fig. 1.12). Colonial craftsmen turned and joined table bases that looked very like those in rural England yet routinely produced tops that were larger. The roomy tabletops, one or two boards that overhung the frames, gave many American tables their distinctive appearance. That spreading reach, that flare, came to characterize some tea tables, such as the Saywards' walnut tea table (see fig. 8.3) and a mahogany example made in the area of Wethersfield, Connecticut, some forty or fifty years later (fig. 8.5). In contrast, the top on the *k'ang* table was contained within the frame, and not all American tea tables had broadly reaching tops. Stylish urban examples were very like their English contemporaries, each looking like a lipped rectangular tea tray placed on a four-legged base made to its dimensions. Sayward's mahogany table made in the Boston

Figure 8.6. Tea table, mahogany and pine, H: 28⅝"; W: 36"; D: 22⅜". Robert Harrold, Portsmouth, 1765–1775. (Carnegie Museum.) The Chinese touches favored in the 1760s and 1770s were straight legs and fretwork carvings.

Figure 8.7. Tea table, Philadelphia, 1760–1790. (Israel Sack.) The so-called birdcage beneath the tabletop permits the top both to rotate when in use and to flip to a vertical position for storage. Such tables were prized for the carvings on the legs and the pillar and for the dished and scalloped top.

style (at the left in the parlor view, fig. 7.6), the Philadelphia tea table in the Winterthur Museum setting (see fig. 8.2), and the Portsmouth table by Robert Harrold (fig. 8.6) all look like trays on legs or stands. In period terms they were "square," which referred to the shape of the corners.

Other tea tables, such as a splendidly carved Philadephia example (fig. 8.7), were round and looked like circular tea trays set on tripods. A plainer example sat in the corner of the Saywards' parlor (see fig. 7.6). The round Philadelphia table permitted the hostess to rotate the top—all the better for serving. Round tops also could be flipped up vertically, and after teatime the table could be retired near the wall.

On square tea tables with overhanging tops, the edges of the top usually form a lip or railing to protect the expensive tea set. The *k'ang* table has a slight lipped edge. A tray-edge molding, now missing, originally outlined the Saywards' square walnut table. Molding rims its mahogany replacement and the Philadelphia example laden with china. The enthusiastic scalloping of the edge on the Wethersfield table inhibited the cabinetmaker from adding a molding. Robert Harrold used galleried edges to enclose the tops of his tea tables. Many round examples were dished out on a lathe, many square ones had an applied molded edge, but a scalloped and dished round top (as on fig. 8.7) required considerable carving after the lathe work, making such tables lavish and expensive.

A TABLE AT CENTER STAGE

The tea table in the parlor was brought forward from the wall at teatime. When the party gathered in the parlor, it was called a "tea party." On many occasions a woman served tea in her bedchamber. There, too, the table took center stage, even upstaging the fully hung bed or perhaps an elegantly japanned high chest. Mrs. Washington served tea to Latrobe on her piazza (see fig. 4.5).

Four-sided tables—often called "china tables" for their function, not their design—might be set before or near the fire, thereby placing the tea equipage in the middle of things. Often a marriageable daughter sat at the table and poured; she and the table were at the center of the festivities. Because guests could approach from here or there, square tea tables were designed to be seen from any angle, as round tea tables were, and finished on all four sides. All four table rails featured the same S-curved outlines or rococo carvings.

The way the rails of tea tables were finished makes it clear to anyone reading them that china tables were not meant to sit shyly off against the wall for long. Yet dining tables still folded up as if almost to disappear against the wall, as the one in the Sayward parlor did. Card tables, too, folded up to stand close to the wall. A round Federal table became a demi-lune table against the wall (such as that on the cabinetmaker's label, fig. 8.8). Round tea tables had tops that could tilt for the same reason. With the round top in its vertical position, the table retreated, perhaps into the corner of the room. The permanently open china table, constructed so very differently, was distinct from its more retiring brethren.

After 1815 a succession of tables were made to stand open permanently, usually as the focal point in the very center of a room: one in the dining room, one in the parlor, and one in the library. In the dining room, the era of foldable, removable tables (such as the set of three, fig. 6.6) continued long after the wall-hugging sideboard had decisively established the function of the room, ending only with the permanently open dining table of the mid-nineteenth century. That was when the crumb cloth no longer made sense. No one removed a table such as the one depicted in the middle of the furniture showroom (fig. 8.9). In their Brooklyn parlor, the Bullards sat at a centered table (see fig. 5.8). The center of the Morses' drawing room in Portland had an imposing Louis XIV table (see fig. 3.10). The center table in many parlors and libraries held the room's principal lamp (see the centered library table, fig. 3.9) and became the family's gathering place, not unlike the way the tea table had claimed the central role in the parlor more than a century before.

CHANGING DRINKS AND TABLES

Drink tables have come down in the world. As popular social drinks changed, so did their tables.[8] The American parlor or living room of the early twentieth century remained the scene of parties, but rarely tea parties. A lower table became fashionable because the seats on parlor suites were lower. The tabletop was surrounded by a protective molding like that of the tea table. However, instead of being centered in the room, it was centered in front of the sofa, and in honor of the drink commonly served after dinner it was called a coffee table. Many had oval tray-tops of glass.

Coffee tables occasionally held coffee cups, but they were not the raison d'être. People expected, needed, a table that would permanently stand away from the wall for an designs. featuring pagoda roofs, a plethora of filigree, and straight legs.

Mid-eighteenth-century English design books, and American craftsmen as well, promoted the "Chinese," "Modern," and "Gothic" tastes. The arch of the stretchers on Harrold's table are drawn out versions of the arch in his "Gothic" chair splats (see fig. 7.4). Harrold captured the spirit of genuine Chinese tables in the straight skirt he gave the table rail. He put "Chinese" filigree along its length and placed echoes of it as brackets between the rails and legs. The overall impression was Chinese; as Denker says, "It was not the details but the overall impression that justified the designation 'in the Chinese taste.'" English furniture in the Chinese taste came to America, New Hampshire's Governor John Wentworth brought such a parlor suite with him in 1767, but his high-style examples did not become models for American craftsmen or their customers.

"Chinese taste" in Britain was sufficiently Chinese by midcentury to suggest that the English were having more contact with Chinese objects. They had far better models than Stalker and Parker did. The connection was through the few Englishmen to have contact with China, the tea traders. Seafaring merchants, captains of trading vessels, were permitted only restricted access to a select few Chinese merchants, with whom they conducted business at the edge of Canton Harbor. They did not visit Chinese homes.

On occasion, a trader acted as a design courier, carrying English Georgian design to China. The Chinese, however, did not borrow from English design. Rather, a few English noblemen ordered furniture to be made by Chinese craftsmen in the English style. These wares were either copied from English examples taken to China or, more likely, made from drawings. Perhaps such a trader was the conduit of designs in both directions; perhaps one sketched the Chinese furniture he saw.

Someone saw something.

CABRIOLES AND HORSEBONES

Tea traders who sketched may explain the Chinese fashion of the mid-eighteenth century. But what of the earlier style with cabriole legs and S-curves? Where did English cabinetmakers learn of Ming design?

Maybe a tea trader brought home a *k'ang* table to use as a tea tray. Or perhaps a Portuguese, trading out of Macao, acquired a Ming *k'ang* table or, having seen one, carefully sketched it. That could have been in the late seventeenth century, and by the early eighteenth century the fashion would have become firmly established.

Looking at the Saywards' walnut tea table (see fig. 8.3), one might think it was copied from a Ming *k'ang* table. Not a shred of evidence, however, suggests that either the owner or the maker, the joiner Samuel Sewall of York (1724–1814), ever saw a Ming table.[11] Such a connection was most improbable.

The impression that a Chinese table was a direct design source is strong at both the cabrioles, with their sharp corners, and the skirt. The Chinese used a sharp crease down the corner of their cabriole legs. Among the English, creased cabrioles were an early fashion, and they remained popular north of Boston even after English and other American cabrioles were rounded. The older style, the creased cabriole, was more genuinely Chinese.

In the late seventeenth century, the English gained an important Chinese connection through a royal marriage when the Portuguese princess Catherine of Braganza arrived to marry Charles II in 1662. Among the splendors she introduced to Britain (along with the misnamed "Spanish" foot) may have been furniture that was either Chinese or inspired by the Chinese. Her countrymen had been at Macao since 1557, trading with Canton. She could have introduced a style at court that then filtered down in British society. Some fine English chairs of about 1700 had square-cornered cabrioles.[12] The first cabrioles that Americans ever saw may well have been this variety. America's early cabrioles may be the fruit of the Chinese-Portuguese link at Macao, a Portuguese-British marriage, and the London-colonial trade.

"Cabriole" (a variant is "capriole") took its name from *capra*, Italian for "goat." Funny. When the cabriole leg first became popular in America, it was called "horsebone." "Hoofs" and "fetlocks" are distinct on the Sayward's walnut tea table and the other tables in the house.[13] Some early "horsebones" looked even more anatomically horsy.

The period names have animalistic connotations, yet in 1996 Jonathan Prown and Richard Miller, furniture scholars, saw high

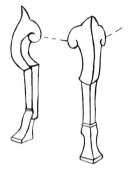

chests on cabriole legs as bipeds, "quite human," emitting sexual messages—sometimes masculine, sometimes feminine.[14] Many people see curves as feminine and rectilinear design as masculine. They could perhaps see curves as relaxed and the rectilinear as uptight. Perhaps it would be still better to see cabrioles as Ming and straight legs as Ch'ing or Manchu (1644–1912).

When the French, customers of Portuguese and Dutch merchants in the Asian trade, adopted the cabriole, they rounded the design. The English followed the stylish French, curving the Chinese crease. In northern New England, cabrioles tended to retain the sharp creases at the knee, even on the legs of tripod table bases. On Sayward's walnut table, the crisp crease vanishes into a rounded leg to create the horsebone.

The design of the table rail or skirt echoes in outline the *k'ang* skirt. Since the lines on Chinese furniture were elegantly simple, and simplicity was a Chinese far more than a European characteristic, the plain contours on Sayward's modest table make it most authentically Chinese. The skirt of the Chinese table, however, is pulvinated, or swelled. The maker of the Pennsylvania table (see fig. 8.2) also used that feature; however, he embellished the swelled surface with carved curves.

The maker of the Connecticut tea table (fig. 8.5) also strayed from the simple Chinese lines. Like most of his fellow cabinetmakers, he used a three-part design for the skirt, a design created for the skirt of a high chest. The skirt on his tea table is much like that on the one-piece trunk lids and broad, overhanging tabletops. In the eighteenth century, engaged in a robust timber trade with colonies to the south, they began to use fine primary woods lavishly. In making blockfronts, cabinetmakers seemed almost to squander the wood, making each drawerfront from a slab three times as thick as a drawerfront had to be.

American cabinetmakers, having succeeded in getting the board timbers that Evelyn had wanted, had only mastered the skill of building cases of boards, cabinetry, at the end of the seventeenth century. Yet by the late 1730s they seemed to have tired of flat boards and took to sculpting case furniture. Perhaps it was seeing all that wood in their forests. With blockfronts, the cabinetmakers looked again to carving parts of cases, a tradition that went back to working with solid logs. Perhaps they looked at the bulbous and sculptured cases that had remained a part of Europe's carved furniture tradition. By then, however, Europeans had to stack wood together to create the block to be carved. Not so Americans.

The blockfront led the way, and soon cabinetmakers were also making cases in more sculptured shapes that used wood opulently:

- the bombé: a bulbous case whose façade and sides undulate from top to bottom, bulging at the bottom;
- the oxbow, or reverse serpentine: a shape whose façade smoothly undulates sideways—out, in, and out;
- the serpentine: a Federal façade that undulates in, out, and in; and
- the bowfront: a rounded Federal façade.

In creating each new façade, the cabinetmakers smoothed the way for the next design. It was as if each sculptural form saw the next one coming. The oxbow smoothed the blocked front into a meandering line, which led to the serpentine by a simple reversal of the curve. Then came the bow, a simple arc. Each shape appeared progressively lighter. Cabinetmakers produced oxbows, serpentines, and bowfronts into the 1800s, by which time the best mahogany was long gone. Eventually they constructed serpentine and bowed drawerfronts from stacked rather than solid wood, facing the stacks with veneer.

Connecticut cabinetmakers used local cherry; elsewhere in New England cabinetmakers briefly used walnut, which had to be shipped from the southern colonies, but they soon switched to mahogany from the Caribbean. Most swelled cases by far are mahogany, the wood of the Boston chest (fig. 9.3). The fashion originated, however, with walnut, the wood of the Portsmouth high chest (fig. 9.4)

Blockfronts are the oldest of the shaped cases. Boston cabinetmakers were working on the design in the late 1730s and made some of walnut. On the other hand, the earliest dated bombé, a form made only in coastal Massachusetts, is a 1753 mahogany desk and bookcase; there is little reason to believe that the form much predates that time.

The earliest dated blockfront, inscribed 1738, was made of walnut by a Boston father and son, Job Coit, Sr. and Jr. Their signed and dated desk and bookcase shows that they were

Bombé

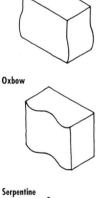

Oxbow

Serpentine

Bowfront

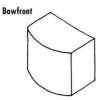

still tackling some construction difficulties.[11] Whether they were originating the blockfront, introducing it to Boston, or simply developing the design they saw elsewhere is not known. By signing and dating their case, however, at the time when craftsmen rarely signed furniture, they were perhaps showing the pride of an innovator or introducer.

Joseph Davis, a native of Portsmouth and the maker of the blockfront high chest (fig. 9.4), was an apprentice to the senior Coit in 1726. Having gone to Boston to learn his trade, Davis returned to Portsmouth in 1733 or 1734, before the Coits got to struggling with blocked construction. Clearly, he had not learned blocking from Coit. A note on prideful signing: Davis signed a veneered high chest and the blockfront dressing table that matches the high chest. Unfortunately he omitted the dates.

The Portsmouth high chest by Coit's one-time apprentice may predate the dated Coit case. Davis's blocking seems more basic, more architectural. In general, cabinetmakers cut their blocked drawerfronts from a thick slab of wood—a single solid slab—or from a thick piece made deeper at the center with a glued board. But not Davis. He applied his blocking to flat drawerfronts. Where other blocked cases were recessed in the center, Davis applied center blocking to the lower case. On the upper case, his two applied blocks suggest a concave center in the space between. Looking at a Davis blockfront—high chest or dressing table—we see elemental blocking.

And his legs look like early cabrioles: those

Figure 9.3 Chest of drawers, mahogany and white pine, original brass, H: 30⅞"; W: 34⅝"; D: 21". Shop of Benjamin Frothingham, Charlestown (now part of Boston), 1755–1765. It may date from the 1764 marriage of two wealthy Bostonians, Samuel A. Otis and Elizabeth Gray. (Society for the Preservation of New England Antiquities.) The blocking on small cases was often rounded, while that on large Boston cases was like that on the Salem desk (fig. 1.10).

on one blocked and pilastered dressing table terminate in "Spanish feet." The legs on the illustrated Davis high chest are replacements—a third set—replicas of the surviving legs on the matching dressing table. The original legs were lost and their replacements inaccurate. One can look at the massive case on its slender curving legs and see why many cabrioles came

Figure 9.4. High chest, walnut and pine, H: 74⅛"; W: 47⅜"; D: 25½". Joseph Davis, Portsmouth, 1735–1740. (Diplomatic Reception Rooms.) Davis signed the matching dressing table, featuring a corresponding carved fan, blocking, and corner pilasters. The cabriole legs on the high chest are replacements copied from those on the matching dressing table.

to be severed (see page x). The current legs on Davis's signed veneered high chest are also replacements.

Blockfronts were always premier cases and always made of the prime wood of the place and time. Davis made his blockfronts of black walnut. A few walnut blockfronts, some with inlay, were made in Boston as well, one signed by a Richard Walker, a similar one dated 1739.[12] Apparently, when the Coits, Walker, and Davis made their blockfronts, mahogany was not yet widely available.

FROM CLASSICAL GREECE TO AMERICAN CLASSIC

Blockfronts also speak of baroque grandeur and classical architecture. The robust architectural character of Davis's Portsmouth high chest is like that of late-seventeenth-century English interiors. Davis's cornice and waist moldings are essentially Georgian woodwork. (Compare them to the Georgian moldings and cornice above the arch in the Royall house entry, fig. 6.3, and note the flanking pilasters.)

Davis's blockfronts feature pilasters, which people read as columns. Eighteenth- and nineteenth-century Americans loved columns and pilasters—Greek, Roman, or Palladian—seeing them simply as classical and fashionable. Their Georgian houses had columns and pilasters of all sorts placed here and there. Americans mixed up the classical orders—Doric, Ionic, Corinthian, Tuscan. If Asher Benjamin (1773–1845), the American architect and writer of architectural books, could design his own order, so could every joiner and carpenter. And they did. Davis's pilasters and hefty cornice must have sounded exactly the right message in Portsmouth, where architectural components were important to the town's crafts and a significant part of its timber export trade.

Although Davis's high chest is not alone in its architectural character, it is exceedingly so, and remarkably structural.[13] The fluted pilasters at the corners are visual supports for the ends of the massive cornice. Perhaps we should read the applied blocking as secondary pilasters. The cornice treats them as such, capping them in the same way it caps the pilasters. The weighty molding seems to necessitate additional supports across the façade. The upper case is an abstract, flat-roofed building.

In the twentieth century, classical columns and pilasters may seem anything but abstract designs, however they were just that—wonderful abstractions of sturdy trees. The shaft of a Tuscan column was an abstract tree trunk holding up a roof; the fluted shaft of an Ionic or Corinthian column a cluster of trees, bound together on top and bottom, the bindings becoming the column's capital and base. On Corinthian capitals, carved greenery suggested some leaves remaining just above the trunks.

However we read pilasters and the façades of blockfront cases, the pilaster enthusiasts of Portsmouth must have seen Davis's high chest as a small piece of architecture.

A TALE OF THREE CITIES

A third message from blockfront design is about the benefits of America's being a place of places. The several colonies had separate political identities. A walnut shipment entering Boston Harbor from a southern colony was as much an import as the mahogany shipped from the Caribbean. England had London at the core of its design; France had Paris; the colonies, however, had several distinctive urban centers of style. In America the blockfront could originate, develop, and be honed in discrete design climates. Omitting the blockfronts of the Connecticut River valley—variations of the Boston blockfront that tell yet other stories—we concentrate on three ports: Portsmouth, Boston, and Newport.

Davis's architecturally complex case is not sophisticated. His cabinetry is standard for one who learned his trade in Boston. If Boston craftsmen had been making blockfronts at the time Davis left, in 1733 or 1734, he would have known more about the design and construction of Boston blockfronts than his cases indicate. Instead his blocking, his simply applied boards, made a design statement that endured in his town. Portsmouth people continued to like flat blocking. Portsmouth blockfronts were finally identified in 1982 because, while searching for examples related to a small chest of drawers with flat blocking and a bit of a Portsmouth history, Brock Jobe and I found that similarly blocked chests had firm Portsmouth connections.[14]

Most furniture scholars have believed that the blockfront originated in Boston. I wonder. It seems possible to me that Davis found blocking or initiated it in Portsmouth. The blockfront idea could have started in a town in which the lumber trade was king. In 1715, John Drew (d. 1738), a joiner from England, arrived in Portsmouth and built glorious houses with splendid Palladian interiors. He may also have made some case furniture. Then, shortly before Drew's death, Davis arrived back in the midst of all that lumber and Drew's woodwork.

Davis cases can be read as proclaiming the wonders of the region. Portsmouth annually exported pine boards by the hundreds of thousands of feet and traded in primary woods. Sawmills were at the center of the area's economy. The colonial governor, living in Portsmouth, carried the title "Surveyor of the King's Woods." Since boards were Portsmouth's commodity, no wonder a Portsmouth cabinetmaker put boards on his case façades.

Wherever the blockfront began, the design certainly was developed in the late 1730s in Boston, where cabinetmakers made blocking integral to the case. The cabinetmakers of Boston and Salem, to which many Bostonians moved during the 1775–1776 British siege of Boston, produced blockfronts for local consumption by prosperous merchants and for export. They made small blocked chests of drawers and hefty cases—double chests, desks, and secretaries—but not blockfront high chests and dressing tables as Davis did.

By 1760, having looked at Boston blockfronts, the cabinetmakers in Newport adopted the design: they saw the potential and perfected the form. Thus the blockfront reached its apex in the hands of Newport's Christopher Townsend (1701–probably 1787), John God-

religious diversity that resulted. The entry hall mottoes proved successful. While America eschewed one established faith, the country proved to be decidedly theistic.

At the end of the nineteenth century, the Romanesque Revival and a resurgence of the Gothic helped the Arts and Crafts Movement link handwork to godliness, an antidote for the evil incarnate in machines, machine work, and replication. The movement began and flourished in England and made a flurry among Anglophiles and well-to-do Americans, but it was far less important here. Americans, instead, snapped up what machines produced and even machines themselves—from an automobile in the garage to an electric can opener on the kitchen counter.

Our other great faith has been in our country, in what was often seen as its moral character forged in an idealized past epitomized by neoclassicism. A 1994 addition to American utopias was Celebration, Florida, the Walt Disney Company's idea of an all-American town. Celebration promised neoclassical motifs and apple pie images in its plans for houses and apartments. The developers, seeing Celebration as inclusive, were against gating the community. The architectural scholar Vincent Scully lauded the idea as creating a small town, the sort of community that was "destroyed in large part by the automobile. Celebration," he said, "grows out of the way people want to live." [21]

Disney architects and designers created houses in styles popular in the Southeast before World War II—Classical Revival, Victorian, "coastal," Colonial Revival, Mediterranean, or French—and created a stylebook of over a hundred pages, governing every architectural element of the houses. The patterns illustrate friendly, large, open porches. In bug country, which central Florida is, these probably will eventually be screened, but without porches, how could the town look American and wholesome?

Fifty miles from Seattle, between Tacoma and Olympia, another community was rising featuring "porches in the front, garages in the rear . . . village green and town hall." [22] The developers took the ideas for their new town from the old town, Du Pont, Washington, a two-hundred-home company town of the 1920s and 1930s, now a national historic district.

A century after Wharton and Codman sought a moral environment for children through design, Americans took the same approach. At Celebration, a potential customer and mother of three thought that the town would provide "a more wholesome and moral environment for kids." To William Morrish, the director of the Design Center for American Urban Landscape at the University of Minnesota, designing a new town, "a new utopia," is "a great American tradition: 'Next time we'll do it better.' " [23] Optimism is as American as porches and neoclassical revivals.

URBAN LIVING

The wealthy have long enjoyed a city pied-à-terre to augment their country homes. Harriet Manigault's family lived in a house in Philadelphia in addition to its country seat, and the Carolina Manigaults removed from their indigo plantations to Charleston houses.

In the nineteenth century, apartment buildings were common in large European cities. But not yet in American cities. This was a nation of homeowners. With escalating immigration and Civil War dislocation, however, American cities became places for transients, new arrivals who had yet to establish themselves in a home. Better-off transients lived in boardinghouses, for some six months at a time. Maria Morse, who wrote of installing carpets in her new home, was boarding in the nation's capital. The poorer sort lived in tenements, small divisions of urban housing, some no larger than a room. My grandparents took their chest of six drawers for five children to a tenement apartment and then on to other, larger apartments. Boardinghouses and tenements were both very temporary.

Rental apartments were barely more so. The American apartment house emerged in the 1860s and 1870s, but the ideal remained a single-family house. In 1997, almost 66 percent of householders owned their homes.[24] The ideal, brought to America by the rural English settlers, was pursued even in crowded cities like New York, where some poorly constructed houses went up in the late nineteenth century on city lots that were amazingly narrow—perhaps 25 feet wide by 100 feet deep—with windows only along the narrow front and rear. Few urban workers managed to have a house, although affluent families clung to their ideal.

In the 1890s, an apartment was home for most people in New York City. Some saw it as a moral improvement over boarding. Parents and children sat together for dinner at their own table rather than at that of their host in a boardinghouse. Americans saw moral benefits in housekeeping. When urban land values forced vertical living and market factors fostered maximizing livable spaces, some reformers saw urban apartments as efficient and ideal. To people familiar with apartments in European cities, one's own apartment was a joy, a place to establish a home. Many planners and architects saw apartments as a viable substitute for single-family houses.

An apartment house in an American city was not like one in Paris. In Paris, the relationships among residents were clearly defined. Artisans lived in upper-story apartments, aristocrats on the lower floors. Were these vertically separated neighbors to meet on the stairs, each knew how to act; their behavior and relationship had been established for generations. Not so in America. Apartment houses held families of similar means and station in society.

While to some Americans in the early twentieth century a city apartment was desirable, to others, including immigrants, the single-family residence remained the goal. Italian immigrants sought houses in New York City as quickly as they could, as did the Irish. Jews, seldom landowners in Europe, were content to live in apartments. Their forebears in *shtetls* may actually have aspired to apartments in Warsaw, Berlin, Vienna, or Paris. Only in the mid-twentieth century did later generations see the American dream in terms of house ownership. Aided by the GI Bill after World War II and encouraged by the movement toward green space, they found their ideal in suburban communities.

Meanwhile, Walter Gropius had left Nazi Germany and the Bauhaus in 1937 for America and Harvard, soon to be joined by Marcel Breuer. Ludwig Mies van der Rohe came later, settling in Chicago. Gropius designed his own home (1938) in Lincoln, Massachusetts, a two-story house so compact it was almost an apartment on open land: it had no basement, a gallery-kitchen as narrow as one in a European apartment, rooms that led to rooms, and an unroofed terrace on the second story, very like an apartment terrace. Later, the Gropiuses added a first-floor porch overlooking their land, after the idea of the American porch affected their sensibilities.

The Gropius house, now a museum operated by the Society for the Preservation of New England Antiquities, features glass brick and chrome details and looks like an apartment in prewar Vienna, where, until 1938, wealthy Austrians lived almost regally in spacious apartments with servants—maids, a governess, and a cook at the least—and with much of the interior splendor of a grand house.

The Bauhaus architects—Gropius, Breuer, and Mies—plunked down on American soil the several elements of international design: the chrome details and glass bricks, the Breuer and Mies chairs. Literally "down." Their designs became part of new, compact, often flat-roofed homes even more than part of apartment living.

PUBLIC OR PRIVATE, NAUGHTY OR NICE

Remember the room-beyond-room floor plan that Latrobe would have welcomed in New Orleans but that Americans would not adopt? Edith Wharton, or her character Newland Archer in *Age of Innocence*, considered it "in flagrant violation of all the New York proprieties." The novel, published in 1920, was about life in the 1870s and captured a nineteenth-century American attitude that continued into the twentieth. Bedrooms and beds should be out of sight. But, from a sitting room, Archer saw beyond an open doorway with its "(looped-back yellow damask portiere) the unexpected vista of a bedroom with a huge low bed . . . and a toilet-table with frivolous lace flounces and a gilt-framed mirror."[25]

Archer was startled by the "foreign-ness" of the arrangement, a "stage-setting of adultery," and thought immediately of France. Europe had such "architectural incentives to immorality," where "women with lovers lived in the wicked old societies, in apartments with all the rooms on one floor." No wonder Hess hid his parlor bed and the maker of the folding bed (fig. 9.9) hid his in such an amazingly realistic upright piano case.[26]

By the mid-nineteenth century, Americans no longer received guests in bedrooms. Gone were the expensively draped beds of earlier centuries. Americans even forgot that for centuries European lords sat, surrounded by cushions, in their manorial beds to receive petitions from underlings, at times kept at some remove by a rope railing across the bedchamber at the

Figure 9.9. Folding piano-bed, closed and opening, ca. 1870. (Ex collection of the late Elinor Merrell.)

base of the bed. The French were better at remembering holding court from bed. *Lit*, French for "bed." led to *lit de justice* for a formal session of parliament. which was named for the luxurious sofa-seat—"bed of justice"— on which the French king sat at such sessions.

THERE'S A BED IN THE ____

When Scandinavians and Dutch came to America they gave up their traditions of built-in beds. of box-beds behind cupboard doors. Swedish immigrants had adopted the American bed by 1869. when Oliver Stephenson wrote home to suggest that Swedish quilts could not be used here "where the beds are much larger." Most nineteenth-century American beds were still large and impressive.

Others. however, were hidden. Most of the folding sort were in rooms where they might have been spied by some Newland Archer. Many folding beds were simple and folded up under a mantel to look like a fireplace, providing not merely an extra bed but also an allusion to a hearth and a display shelf, both much coveted.

Some folding beds were bedroom pieces. perhaps in a small room that occasionally became a guest room. Commander and Mrs. Robert E. Peary, living in Washington. D.C., owned an early-twentieth-century chiffonier–folding bed (fig. 9.10). The Arctic explorer's wife. according to family tradition. gave birth to their son. his namesake. in the folding bed.

Americans took to calling such hidden beds, including those built into cases that looked like something else. Murphy beds. In the early twentieth century, the term was usually applied to beds built into the wall. ap-

MUSICAL HEARTHS

In the nineteenth century, pianos were the prime American hearths(fig. 9.12), therefore Hess's disguise and the piano-bed (fig. 9.9) that really looked the part. In 1867, the *Atlantic Monthly* reported that "almost every couple that sets up housekeeping on a respectable scale considers a piano only less indispensable than a kitchen range." President Cleveland opined about Americans and pianos, "In many a humble home throughout the land, the piano has gathered about it the most sacred and tender association."[29]

Families found a piano indispensable to their homes, piano-playing indispensable to their social lives. Piano music accompanied homely everyday moments as well as fancy parties. At the start of the nineteenth century, piano music was a constant in Harriet Manigault's life whichever home the family was occupying. She played piano at home and on visits. She and her sister Charlotte had a standing invitation to Sunday gatherings at the Spanish minister's residence in Philadelphia. At "a delightful evening" in 1813, Harriet "played on the piano for them to dance two or three cotillions, after which we played a game which they call Embassador."[30] Throughout the century, piano performances entertained families and their friends.

Figure 9.13. Mr. and Mrs. Simon in their parlor, photograph by Charles Van Schaick, near Taylor, Wisconsin, ca. 1900. (State Historical Society of Wisconsin.) The Simons pose for their portrait with their most important parlor possession, a reed organ that provides music and display space for photographs, a vase, and books.

Socials permitted young people to show off their accomplishments. The marriageability of a young woman depended on her piano-playing. A young man's skill at the keyboard afforded him the best possible marriage. The piano was the locus for courting, and books defined how a man should escort a woman to the piano and how they should court there.

To serve the demand, piano manufacturing boomed. In 1909, 364,545 pianos were made in the United States by almost three hundred firms, including some of the largest in the world. Steinway (founded in 1853 by a German immigrant family), Chickering, Mason and Hamlin, Story and Clark, Aeolean, and Baldwin were the Sonys of their day. By 1995, however, fewer than 100,000 pianos were made in America. But pianos last, and about 800,000 secondhand pianos were traded. The piano is still a presence in an American home.

Vanity had a large role in piano purchases in the nineteenth century. Appearance—home

15. Fall/winter issue, p. 63.
16. Ibid. pp. 56–57, 62.
17. Gloag, *Social History of Furniture Design*, pp. 20, 67.
18. Illustrated in *History of Technology* (Oxford: Clarendon Press, 1957). Vol. II, p. 190.

Chapter 4: The Peripatetic Porch

1. The Historic Structure Report, Old State House (Boston: Society for the Preservation of New England Antiquities, 1977), citing the WPA report on the building for the bill.
2. Roger G. Kennedy, *Architecture, Men, Women and Money in America, 1600–1860* (New York: Random House, 1985), pp. 68, 71.
3. Elisabeth Garrett, "The American Home," *Antiques*, December 1985, vol.127, n. 6, p. 1215, quoting *Travels in Some Parts of North America in the Years 1804, 1805, 1806* (Philadelphia, 1812), p. 243.
4. Kennedy, *Architecture*, p. 61.
5. Hugh Morrison, *Early American Architecture* (New York: Oxford University Press, 1952), p. 172.
6. Kennedy, *Architecture*, p. 63, quotes Harold D. Eberlein and Cortlandt van Dyke Hubbard, *Historic Houses of the Hudson Valley* (New York: Architectural Book Publishing Co., 1942), p. 48.
7. Philip D. Curtin, *The Atlantic Slave Trade; A Census* (Madison: University of Wisconsin Press, 1969), p. 143.
8. Edward Kimber, "Observations in Several voyages and travels in America in the year 1736," *William and Mary Quarterly*, 1st ser., vol. 15, 1906–7, p. 148.
9. John Michael Vlach, *Back of the Big House* (Chapel Hill: University of North Carolina Press, 1993), p. 165.
10. Vlach, *The Afro-American Tradition in Decorative Arts* (Cleveland: Cleveland Museum of Art, 1978), p. 138.
11. Curtin, *Atlantic Slave Trade*, p. 228.
12. Susan Denyer, *African Traditional Architecture* (London: Heinemann, 1978), on the Tikar and the Bamilék; Paul Oliver, ed. *Shelter in Africa* (London: Barrie & Jenkins, 1971), for the baKosi of Cameroon.
13. Kennedy, *Architecture*, p. 68.
14. Garrett, "American Home," p. 1215, quoting *Travels in Some Parts of North America*, p. 243.
15. Scully, *American Architecture and Urbanism*.
16. *New York Times*, July 9, 1987, p. C1.
17. *New York Times*, July 4, 1996, p. C5.

Chapter 5: A Hole in the Wall

1. Manigault, *Diary*, p. 106.
2. Martineau, *Retrospect*, p. 84.
3. Albert Manucy, *The Houses of St. Augustine: 1565–1821* (Gainesville: University Press of Florida, 1992), p. 31, quoting John Bartram, *Diary of a Journey*, pp. 52, 55.
4. Ibid., pp. 31, 122.
5. *The Diary of Samuel Sewall* (New York: Farrar, Straus, 1973), vol. 2, p. 831.
6. Frederick Law Olmsted, *The Cotton Kingdom: A Selection*

(Indianapolis: Bobbs-Merrill, 1971), p. 61.
7. *Diary of Samuel Sewall*, vol. 2, pp. 621–22.
8. Olmsted, *Cotton Kingdom*, p. 64.
9. *Manigault Diary*, p. 30.
10. Ibid. p. 7.
11. Benjamin Count Rumford, *The Complete Works* (Boston, n.d.), vol. 4, p. 106. Cited by Wolfgang Schivelbusch, *Disenchanted Night: The Industrialization of Light in the Nineteenth Century*, translated by Angela Davies (Berkeley: University of California Press), 1988.
12. Edith Wharton and Ogden Codman, Jr., *The Decoration of Houses* (New York: Norton, 1978), a reprint of the 1902 ed., first published in 1897, p. 126.

Chapter 6: Over the Threshold and Through the Rooms

1. Danckaerts, *Journal*, p. 255.
2. Ibid., p. 256.
3. Cummings, *Inventories*, p. 41.
4. Olmsted, *Cotton Kingdom*, p. 168.
5. Cummings, *Inventories*, p. 93.
6. *Diary of Samuel Sewall*, vol. 2, entry for Jan. 15, 1716, p. 810.
7. Cummings, *Inventories*, pp. 92—93.
8. Ibid., p. 201.
9. *Diary of Samuel Sewall*, vol. 2, pp. 621–22.
10. Ibid., p. 622.
11. Cummings, *Inventories*, p. 245.
12. Martineau, *Retrospect*, pp. 37, 258.
13. Manigault, *Diary*, p. 61.
14. Olmsted, *Cotton Kingdom*, p. 144.
15. John Fowler and John Cornforth, *English Decoration in the Eighteenth Century* (London: Barrie & Jenkins, 1974), p. 67, quoting *Works in Architecture of Robert and James Adam I* (1773), Plate V.
16. Garrett, *At Home*, p. 84.
17. Ibid., p. 85.
18. Manigault, *Diary*, pp. 64, 125.
19. Ibid., p. 18.
20. Ibid., p. 10.
21. Benjamin H. Latrobe, *The Journal of Latrobe* (New York: Burt Franklin, 1971 reprint), p. 187.
22. Ibid., p. 210.
23. Cummings, "Architecture to 1820," talk given at the Lyman House, Waltham, Mass., May 18, 1995.
24. Lewis Mumford, *The Brown Decades*, first published in 1931 (New York: Dover, 1955), pp. 6, 8, 109.
25. Louis Sullivan, *The Autobiography of an Idea* (New York: Dover, 1956), pp. 321, 324.
26. *Sears, Roebuck Catalogue, 1897* (New York: Chelsea House, 1968), a facsimile reprint, p. 669.
27. Suellen Hoy, *Chasing Dirt: The American Pursuit of Cleanliness* (New York: Oxford University Press, 1955), p. 92.
28. From an advertisement in *Decorator and Furnisher*, December 1883, by Bruschke & Ricke, Chicago. Illustrated in David A. Hanks, *Innovative Furniture in America from 1800 to the Present* (New York: Horizon Press, 1981), p. 153.
29. J. L. Mott Iron Works, *Mott's Illustrated Catalog of Victorian Plumbing Fixtures for Bathrooms and Kitchens* (New York:

Dover, 1987), a reprint.

30. Hoy, *Chasing Dirt*, p. 170.

31. Latrobe, *Journal*, p. 23.

32. Cummings, "Three Hearths: A Socioarchitectural Study of Seventeenth-Century Massachusetts Bay Probate Inventories," *Old-Time New England*, vol. 75, no. 263 (1997). The lean-to arrived in New England about 1690; the 1687 Boardman house lean-to was added, the 1690s original lean-to at the Cooper-Frost-Austin house had no hearth.

33. Hermann Muthesius, *The English House* (London, 1979), a translation by Janet Seligmann of Muthesius, *Das englische Haus*, 2nd ed. (Berlin, 1908–1911), p. 96.

34. Olmsted, *Cotton Kingdom*, p. 28.

35. Quoted by Vlach, *Back of the Big House*, p. 43.

36. Jane C. Nylander, *Our Own Snug Fireside* (New York: Knopf, 1993), p. 213.

37. Norman R. Yetman, *Life Under the "Peculiar Institution"* (New York: Holt, Rinehart & Winston; 1970), p. 200. For other remembrances of floor sand, see Garrett, *At Home*, p. 98.

Chapter 7: This Is the Place

1. Both 1611 and 1634 are cited as dates of birth for William Searle. I suspect that the man born in 1611 is not our man; 1634 is more in line with the rest of his biography. He was more likely to marry and emigrate young and to borrow money from a contemporary (Dennis) than from a man young enough to be his son.

2. James L. Garvan, "That Little World, Portsmouth," *Portsmouth Furniture*, ed. Brock Jobe (Boston: Society for the Preservation of New England Antiquities, 1993), p. 25.

3. *The Cabinet and Chair-Maker's Real Friend and Companion* (London: Henry Webley, 1765). The chairs descended in the Wentworth family.

4. Alfred Coxe Prime, *The Arts and Crafts in Philadelphia, Maryland, and South Carolina, 1721–1785: Gleanings from Newspapers* (Topsfield, Mass.: Walpole Society, 1929), pp. 175–76.

5. Brock Jobe and Myrna Kaye, *New England Furniture: The Colonial Era* (Boston: Houghton Mifflin, 1984), no. 119, pp. 402–5.

6. "Robert Harrold: Portsmouth Cabinetmaker," *Antiques*, vol. 143, no. 5 (May 1993), pp. 776–83; additional findings, "Addendum: Discovering Portsmouth's Finials," *Maine Antique Digest*, September 1994, p. 11-B; and after the letter from Ohio, "Evidence from Robert Harrold's Hand," *Maine Antique Digest*, August 1995, p. 6-B.

7. Richard C. Nylander, "The Jonathan Sayward House, York, Maine," *Antiques*, September 1979, pp. 571ff.

8. Ibid., p. 571, quoting an 1869 description of the room.

9. Charles Edward Banks, *History of York, Maine* (Boston, 1931), vol. 1, p. 396.

10. There are several labeled pieces. A bureau with columns at side and cheval type glass above in the diplomatic rooms in the State Dept. (80.103) has a paper label in excellent condition, in the right top drawer.

11. Garrett, *At Home*, p. 252, quoting Wainwright family papers at the New York Public Library.

12. Ibid., p. 262, quoting the *London Furniture Weekly*, May 19, 1877.

13. Manigault noted the Baltimore belles: *Diary*, p. 95.

14. Martineau, *Retrospect*, p. 84.

15. Lonn Taylor and David B. Warren, *Texas Furniture: The Cabinetmakers and Their Work* (Austin: University of Texas Press, 1975), p. 326.

16. Olmsted, *Cotton Kingdom*, pp. 174, 175, 188, 189.

17. Yetman, *"Peculiar Institution,"* p. 221.

18. Olmsted, *Cotton Kingdom*, p. 74.

19. Ibid., pp. 198, 199, 200–201.

20. Caroline Mackensen Romberg, *The Story of My Life Written for My Children* (n.p., 1970), cited by Taylor and Warren, *Texas Furniture*, p. 8.

21. Taylor and Warren, *Texas Furniture*, pp. 298, 312, 324.

22. Ibid., pp. 9–10.

23. *New York Times*, January 10, 1997, p. B4, quoting a comment made a "few years ago" by Marylou Whitney.

24. Taylor and Warren, *Texas Furniture*, p. 297.

25. Harriet Martineau, *Society in America*, ed. Seymour Martin Lipset (Gloucester, Mass.: Peter Smith, 1968), p. 161.

26. For Herman Miller, after the late 1980s for Knoll.

Chapter 8: Table Talk

1. For a detailed story, see *In Praise of Hot Liquors: The Study of Chocolate, Coffee and Tea-Drinking 1600–1850*, an exhibition catalogue, text by Peter B. Brown (York [England]: York Civic Trust, 1995).

2. Rodris Roth, *Tea Drinking in 18th-Century America: Its Etiquette and Equipage* (Washington, D.C.: Smithsonian Institution, 1961), Museum Bulletin 225, p. 66, quoting Israel Acrelius, *A History of New Sweden* (Philadelphia, 1874), p. 158, on a visit in the mid-eighteenth century.

3. Mary Caroline Crawford, *Social Life in Old New England* (New York: Grosset & Dunlap, 1914), p. 251, quoting a 1740 letter.

4. Ibid., pp. 252, 254.

5. *Adams Family Correspondence*, L. H. Butterfield, ed. (Cambridge: Harvard University Press / Belknap Press, 1963), *The Adams Papers*, Series II, vol. 2, p. 295.

6. Crawford, *Social Life*, pp. 282–83.

7. John T. Kirk, *American Furniture & the British Tradition to 1830* (New York: Knopf, 1982), p. 136.

8. Gerald W. R. Ward, "The Intersections of Life: Tables and Their Social Role," pp. 14–26, in David L. Barquist, *American Tables and Looking Glasses at Yale University* (New Haven: Yale University Press, 1992), an essay well worth reading.

9. Ellen Paul Denker, *After the Chinese Taste: China's Influence in America, 1730–1930* (Salem, Mass.: Peabody Museum of Salem, 1985), p. 8.

10. Stalker and Parker, published in Oxford in 1688; 1971 reprint with introduction by H. D. Molesworth (London: Alec Triant, 1971).

11. Myrna Kaye, "The Furniture of Samuel Sewall," *Antiques*, Aug. 1985, pp. 276–84.

12. Such a chair is no. 17, "The Bended Back Chair," an exhibition catalogue (London: Barling, 1990).

13. Such as the Sayward dressing table, Jobe and Kaye, *New*